South Asian Archaeology 2007
Special Sessions 2

ALMA MATER STUDIORUM
UNIVERSITÀ DI BOLOGNA

IsIAO
Istituto Italiano per l'Africa e l'Oriente

The Gilund Project: Excavations in Regional Context

Proceedings of the 19th Meeting of the
European Association of South Asian Archaeology
in Ravenna, Italy, July 2007

Edited by

Teresa P. Raczek
Vasant Shinde

BAR International Series 2132
2010

Published in 2016 by
BAR Publishing, Oxford

BAR International Series 2132

South Asian Archaeology 2007, Special Sessions 2
The Gilund Project: Excavations in Regional Context

ISBN 978 1 4073 0673 5

© The editors and contributors severally and the Publisher 2010

The authors' moral rights under the 1988 UK Copyright,
Designs and Patents Act are hereby expressly asserted.

All rights reserved. No part of this work may be copied, reproduced, stored,
sold, distributed, scanned, saved in any form of digital format or transmitted
in any form digitally, without the written permission of the Publisher.

BAR Publishing is the trading name of British Archaeological Reports (Oxford) Ltd.
British Archaeological Reports was first incorporated in 1974 to publish the BAR
Series, International and British. In 1992 Hadrian Books Ltd became part of the BAR
group. This volume was originally published by Archaeopress in conjunction with
British Archaeological Reports (Oxford) Ltd / Hadrian Books Ltd, the Series principal
publisher, in 2010. This present volume is published by BAR Publishing, 2016.

Printed in England

BAR titles are available from:

BAR Publishing
122 Banbury Rd, Oxford, OX2 7BP, UK
EMAIL   info@barpublishing.com
PHONE   +44 (0)1865 310431
FAX   +44 (0)1865 316916
www.barpublishing.com

Table of Contents

List of Figures ii

Chapter 1
Introduction: A Review of the Gilund Excavations and Related Research 1
Vasant Shinde and Teresa P. Raczek

Chapter 2
Development from Mesolithic to Chalcolithic in the Mewar Region of Rajasthan: Contribution of Gilund Excavation 5
Vasant Shinde

Chapter 3
An Overview of the Antiquities from the 1999-2005 Excavations at Gilund, A Chalcolithic Site in Southeast Rajasthan 11
Julie A. Hanlon

Chapter 4
Cultural Developments at the Chalcolithic Site of Gilund, Rajasthan 21
Matthew J. Landt

Chapter 5
An Insight into the Economy of the Chalcolithic People of Gilund 29
Debasri Dasgupta Ghosh

Chapter 6
Contextualising Gilund: A Comparative Analysis of Technology 33
Teresa P. Raczek

Chapter 7
Middle Asian Interconnections at the Turn of the Second Millennium BC: Locating the Foreign Elements in the Gilund Seals and Seal Impressions 41
Marta Ameri

Chapter 8
Indices of Interaction: Comparisons between the Ahar-Banas and Ganeshwar Jodhpura Cultural Complex 51
Uzma Z. Rizvi

List of Figures

3.1 Location and chronology of excavated Ahar Sites in Rajasthan
3.2 Variety of artifacts discovered at Gilund during the 1999-2005 excavations
3.3 Various humped cattle figurines from Gilund
3.4 Stylized cattle figurines from Gilund
3.5 Humped cattle figurines with pointed faces from Gilund
3.6 Humped cow figurine with udders from Gilund
3.7 Round 'decorated pieces' from Gilund
3.8 Early Historic shell bangles from Gilund
3.9 Copper objects from Gilund: 2 rings, 1 kohl stick, and 3 bangle fragments
3.10 Copper objects from Gilund: 1 knife, 1 chisel fragment, and 2 blade fragments
3.11 Copper molds from Gilund
3.12 Vitrified crucible fragments from Gilund
3.13 Iron points and nails from Gilund
4.1 Map of Rajasthan and the surrounding areas highlighting important sites in the region
4.2 Economic variables for cattle, sheep, and goats ranked by kcal/hr
6.1 Core types by raw material and site
6.2 Blade core platform count
7.1 Plan of building with parallel walls and location of sealing bin
7.2 Sealing bin, plan and profile
7.3 Seals reconstructed from seal impressions
7.4 Seal amulets
7.5 Stamps
7.6 Reconstructed amulets
7.7 Seal-amulets and sealings with comparable impressions
7.8 Seal frequency and readable impressions on backs of sealings
7.9 Chronological chart
8.1 Map of Middle Asian Interaction Sphere (MAIS)
8.2 Map of Rajasthan, with districts surveyed underlined
8.3 Map of site locations from 2003 GJCC Survey
8.4 GJCC ceramic assemblages. Ganeshwar Surface Survey, 2000. Reserved Slip ware and Incised ware, Hawa Mahal, Jaipur
8.5 Copper arrowheads from Ganeshwar, 1978-79 Excavations
8.6 Metallurgical analysis of copper materials from Ganeshwar, Rajasthan
8.7 GJCC chronological framework in regional context
8.8 Chronological comparisons with examples used—GJCC in regional context
8.9 Incised ware from Ahar, Period IA
8.10 Incised ware from Balathal
8.11 Incised ware and Reserved Slip ware from Gilund
8.12 Comparison of Incised Ware from Balathal and from Khatha Dhaba
8.13 Arrowheads from Bagor burial, Phase II
8.14 Chronological comparison between Ganeshwar and Bagor

1. Introduction:
A Review of the Gilund Excavations and Related Research

Vasant Shinde
Teresa P. Raczek

The site of Gilund (Rajsamand District, Rajasthan) is a 22 hectare, two mound site situated near the Banas River in southern Rajasthan. First excavated by B. B. Lal of the Archaeological Survey of India (IAR 1959-60), it was recently re-excavated by Deccan College, Post-Graduate and Research Institute and the University of Pennsylvania (Shinde and Possehl 2005, Shinde et al., 2005). Five seasons of research in four separate excavation areas that spanned both mounds was recently concluded in 2005. Over the years, dozens of researchers excavated at the site and were assisted in no small part by about a hundred residents of Gilund village who skilfully dug, screened, and washed artefacts, and accomplished many other essential jobs. With the assistance of an eager group of graduate students, a full analysis of all artefact classes at Gilund have led to new insights into the social, economic, and political organisation of the region. In addition, two major field surveys (Gosh and Rizvi this volume) added to previous work (Dibyopama 2006; Hooja 1988; Misra 1967) and allow us to expand our focus beyond a single site and think about broader regional trends. The results of this research was presented in a session entitled, 'The Gilund Project, 1999-2005: A Comprehensive Review of the Excavations' at the 19th Meeting of the European Association of South Asian Archaeology in Ravenna, Italy in July 2007. The articles presented here elaborate on the original papers and take into account comments and critiques raised during the session in Ravenna.

The site of Gilund appears to have been first occupied prior to the Chalcolithic period (see Shinde this volume). It grew in the Early and Middle Chalcolithic periods and then shrank in the Late Chalcolithic. A very small Historic Period occupation continued on GLD-1, after which time the site was largely abandoned. The excavations revealed a vibrant community during the main occupation that subsisted largely through agro-pastoralism along with craft production. During the excavations, a number of households and workshops as well as a large building in the form of parallel walls were uncovered. Thousands of artefacts were recovered and painstakingly catalogued and analysed.

In order to fully understand the settlement at Gilund, it is necessary to put it into a broader regional context. While hundreds of contemporaneous sites in southern Rajasthan have been identified, only six have been excavated. The site of Bagor (Misra 1973) was first occupied in 5500 BC and continued to be occupied during the Ahar-Banas period, although it differs greatly from most other sites in the region (IAR 1967-68, 41-2; 1968-69, 26-8; 1969-70, 32-4; Misra 1971a, 1973, 1982). The site of Ahar, located near the Aravallis, was the site of another large agro-pastoral community that engaged in craft production (Sankalia et al., 1969; IAR 1954-55: 14-15; IAR 1955-56, 11). Balathal, near Udaipur, was occupied early; it is a unique site with a massive fortified enclosure (Misra et al., 1995; Misra et al., 1997; Shinde et al., 2002). Purani Marmi, adjacent to the Banas River, is a large, shallow, sprawling site (IAR 1957-58; Mohanty et al., 2000). Ojiyana in Bhilwara District is among those sites that are furthest north (Meena and Tripathi 2001, 2001-2002). The excavations of these sites expanded the available datasets for understanding social processes of the region. Outside of southern Rajasthan, Ahar-Banas pottery also extends to the East, into Madhya Pradesh (Chakrabarti 1999; Dhavalikar 2002; Hanlon 2006; Hooja 1988:43; Possehl and Rissman 1992; Sankalia 1979). Recent excavations at Chichali (Mittra and Shivananda 2000) and Eran (Pandey 1982) add to work done at Navdatoli and Kayatha (Ansari and Dhavalikar 1973; Sankalia et al., 1971; Sankalia et al., 1958; Wakankar 1969) to expand the identification of this cultural complex to the South and East. However, at these sites, the presence of Ahar-Banas pottery is limited to specific layers that cover or are covered by layers with material culture not present in the Benas-Berach basin. In all, over 100 sites with Ahar-Banas pottery have been located in southeastern Rajasthan. The Ahar-Banas is just south of the Ganeshwar-Jodhpura Cultural Complex (see Rizvi this volume) and south, west, and north of Indus sites as well.

The most common feature at these sites, and in many cases the defining feature of the Ahar-Banas Cultural Complex, is the white-painted Black and Red ware, especially convex-sided bowls. Other pottery types include Buff ware, imitation Buff-Slipped ware, Reserved Slip ware, Malwa ware, Red wares (including Lustrous Red ware similar to that of Rangpur), and Grey wares (For a full explanation of Ahar-Banas pottery see Deo 1969a; Mishra 2000; Sankalia 1969; Shinde et al., 2002).

In addition to pottery, other common artefacts at Ahar-Banas sites include terracotta bulls (and more rarely cows) (Deo 1969b; Hanlon 2006; Misra et al., 1993); shell bangles; beads of steatite, stone, and terracotta; spindle whorls, sling balls, toy cart wheels, 'gamesmen' (small baked terracotta objects of various sizes), 'hopscotches' (ground pottery sherds), and various kinds of hammerstones and groundstones. Copper slag and copper items including knives, celts, rings, bangles, and kohl sticks are plentiful at some sites but not at others. Microliths show up inconsistently; Bagor and Gilund had plentiful lithics while other sites did not (Misra 1973; Raczek 2007, 2010). Although few copper objects were recovered, they were found throughout the Chalcolithic phase. In addition, a number of crucibles and molds have been found. Seals and seal impressions bear motifs that can be found at other sites in the region and far away (see Ameri this volume).

The excavations reveal that many sites practiced mixed agro-pastoralism and small-scale craft production. Other sites (like Bagor) focused more on animal husbandry. Ethnobotanical remains include rice from Ahar (Vishnu-Mittre 1969); wheat, barley, three varieties of millet, three varieties of lentils, and peas along with wild plant remains from Balathal (Kajale 1996); and a variety of domesticated and wild foods at Bagor (Kashyap 2006). Faunal studies point to the keeping of sheep, goat, cattle, buffalo, and pig (Joglekar *et al.*, 2003; Meadow and Patel 2002; Shah 1969; Thomas 1975, 1977, 1984; Thomas and Joglekar 1996).

The economy at Gilund was also centred on agro-pastoralism and small-scale craft manufacture. In addition to multiple workshop areas, the site held evidence for trade and exchange with other sites in the region as well as with other regions. Such relationships were common throughout the Mewar Plain (Hooja 1988, 1996; Lukacs 2002; Misra 1971b; Possehl 2002; Possehl and Kennedy 1979; Raczek 2007).

As the largest site of the region, Gilund may have served as a political centre (see Shinde this volume). The large architecture in the form of the parallel walls along with administrative sealings found in this area attest to the presence of community leadership and social stratification at the site (Shinde and Possehl 2005). Intriguingly, traces of a thick outer wall were found at both Gilund and Balathal.

The Gilund excavations represent an international collaboration between institutions in the United States and India. Over the course of the five year excavations, dozens of students from India, United States, Canada, Switzerland, Belgium, Italy, United Kingdom, and Japan were trained in archaeological methods. All materials including pottery, lithics, fauna, and small finds have been subjected to thorough and extensive analysis with the goal of answering a number of research questions about social life in the Mewar Plain in the first few millennia BC. A forthcoming site report will present the data from these studies. The papers presented here showcase the methodical work that has been done in and around Gilund for the past several years. Beyond simply categorizing and counting artefacts, these researchers elucidate the social, economic, and political implications of their finds. By systematically testing hypotheses about ancient life in the Mewar Plain they have drawn a number of important conclusions that are simultaneously substantial contributions to the archaeology of this time period and region.

Shinde presents a discussion of the transition from the Mesolithic to the Chalcolithic in southeastern Rajasthan. Joining evidence from Gilund to evidence found at Bagor and Balathal, he argues that the Chalcolithic sites in the region arose from previously established Mesolithic communities. He further postulates that the rise of the Chalcolithic was linked to contact with Harappan peoples, most notably in Gujarat.

Hanlon spent nearly a year carefully curating, cataloguing, and photographing the Gilund small finds, and presents a portion of her research here. Her focus on the zoomorphic terracotta figurines shows the great variety found at Gilund and demonstrates how they are stylistically similar to figurines found at other sites. In addition, her stylistic analysis of other terracotta objects, and objects of stone, shell, copper, iron and steatite also links Gilund to other sites in the region.

Landt analyzed the fauna collection from Gilund in order to determine the kinds of herd management strategies that the ancient residents utilised. He supplements his study with published studies from Bagor and Ahar as well as environmental data which shows variation in rainfall over time. Landt argues that while pastoralists manage risk by maintaining specific species composition of their herds, social values are considered to be just as important as environmental factors to decision making processes.

Dasgupta Ghosh reports on her site catchment analysis of the 10km area immediately surrounding Gilund. During her systematic survey, she found abundant environmental resources for successful agro-pastoralism, hunting, fishing, and craft production. She identified a number of clay pits, lime deposits and quartz outcrops which provided useful resources. Her discussion of craft production indicates that the people of Gilund engaged in trade and exchange.

Raczek presents a comparison of technologies utilised at Gilund and Bagor in order to place Gilund in a broader regional context. She argues that although the day-to-day activities conducted at these sites may have varied, the inhabitants of these two sites shared a common skill set which points to sustained contact and a shared history. Her conclusions are based on a full analysis of the lithic collections from both sites, with a special emphasis on microblade cores.

Ameri takes up the topic of the iconography present on the seals and seal impressions of Gilund as compared to iconography used throughout South Asia and Central Asia. Her study identifies common motifs in Pakistan, Afghanistan, Syria, Turkmenistan and Iran. These motifs span a considerable time frame from possibly as early as 4800 BC to sometime later than 1800 BC.

Finally, Rizvi presents her work on the Ganeshwar-Jodhpura Cultural Complex, which lies to the North of the Ahar-Banas Cultural Complex. She systematically compares the ceramic assemblages of both complexes and also discusses copper arrowheads found in both regions. She finds that early phases of the Ganeshwar-Jodhpura Cultural Complex share commonalities with the Ahar-Banas Cultural Complex and Phase II at Bagor. Her work adds the important element of placing Gilund in a larger regional context.

Acknowledgments

We would like to thank Maurizio Tosi for offering the physical and intellectual space to hold a session on Gilund and related research. We would also like to thank Gregory Possehl for helping to organise the initial session and his support in the compilation of this volume. We thank the Archaeological Survey of India and the Government of India who granted permission for excavation and study of the Gilund artefacts, as well as related survey and collection work presented in this volume. We also thank the State of Rajasthan Department of Archaeology and Museums and the staff at the Government State Museum in Jaipur. Financial support for the excavations was provided by Deccan College, the University of Pennsylvania Museum of Anthropology and Archaeology, the National Science Foundation (NSF INT99-08463), the American Institute of Indian Studies, The University of Pennsylvania Undergraduate Research Fund, and James and Karen Possehl. Pradeep Mehendiratta, Purnima Mehta, and Madhav Bhandare of the American Institute of Indian Studies provided valuable counsel and assistance. We warmly thank the people of Gilund who worked hard during the excavations and helped many of the contributors in this volume conduct their research. We especially thank Girish Vyas and Omji Bohra for their tremendous help at Gilund. We would also like to gratefully acknowledge Ms. Tiffany Black who helped with the technical editing of this volume.

Bibliography

Ansari, Z. D. and M. K. Dhavalikar. 1973. *Excavations at Kayatha*. Pune, Deccan College.

Chakrabarti, D. K. 1999. *India: An Archaeological History: Palaeolithic Beginnings to Early Historic Foundations*. Delhi, Oxford University Press.

Deo, S. B. 1969a. Pottery text. In H. D. Sankalia, S. B. Deo and Z. D. Ansari (eds), *Excavations at Ahar (Tambavati)*, 28-162. Pune, Deccan College.

Deo, S. B. 1969b. Terracotta objects. In H. D. Sankalia, S. B. Deo and Z. D. Ansari (eds), *Excavations at Ahar (Tambavati)*, 176-198. Pune, Deccan College.

Dhavalikar, M. K. 2002. Early farming cultures of Central India. In S. Settar and R. Korisettar (eds), *Prehistory: Archaeology of South Asia*, 253-62. Indian Archaeology in Retrospect, Volume I, S. Settar and R. Korisettar, general editors. Delhi, Manohar and Indian Council of Historical Research.

Dibyopama, A. 2006. *Site Catchment Analysis of Balathal*. Unpublished M. A. Dissertation. Deccan College.

Hanlon, J. A. 2006. *The Gilund Terracottas: A New Look at the Ahar Culture in Rajasthan and Madhya Pradesh*. Unpublished M.Phil. Thesis. University of Cambridge.

Hooja, R. 1988. *The Ahar Culture and Beyond: Settlements and frontiers of 'Mesolithic' and early agricultural sites in south eastern Rajasthan, c. 3rd 2nd Millennia B.C*. British Archaeological Reports International Series 412. Oxford, British Archaeological Reports.

Hooja, R. 1996. Expressing ethnicity and identity: Frontiers and boundaries in pre-history. *The Indian Journal of Social Work* 17(1), 91-114.

Archaeological Survey of India

1954-55. Ahar, District Udaipur, *Indian Archaeology: A Review* (IAR), 14-15.

1955-56. Excavations at Ahar, District Udaipur, *Indian Archaeology: A Review* (IAR), 11.

1957-58. Exploration in Districts Bhilwara, Chitorgarh and Udaipur, *Indian Archaeology: A Review* (IAR), 43-45.

1959-60. Excavations at Gilund, *Indian Archaeology: A Review* (IAR), 41-6.

1967-68. Excavations at Bagor. *Indian Archaeology: A Review* (IAR).

1968-69. Excavations at Bagor. *Indian Archaeology: A Review* (IAR).

1969-70. Excavations at Bagor. *Indian Archaeology: A Review* (IAR).

Joglekar, P., P. K. Thomas and R. K. Mohanty. 2003. Faunal remains from Purani Marmi: A late Ahar Culture settlement in the Mewar region of Rajasthan. *Man and Environment* 28(2), 99-110.

Kajale, M. D. 1996. Palaeobotanical investigations at Balathal: Preliminary results. *Man and Environment* 21(1), 98-102.

Kashyap, A. 2006. *Use-wear and Starch Grain Analysis: An Integrated Approach to Understanding the Transition from Hunting and Gathering to Food Production at Bagor, Rajasthan, India*. Unpublished Ph.D. Dissertation. Michigan State University.

Lukacs, J. R. 2002. Hunting and gathering strategies in prehistoric India: A biocultural perspective on trade and subsistence. In K. D. Morrison and L. Junker (eds), *Forager-Traders in South and Southeast Asia: Long Term Histories*, 41-61. Cambridge, Cambridge University Press.

Meadow, R. H. and A. K. Patel. 2002. From Mehrgarh to Harappa and Dholavira: Prehistoric pastoralism in North-Western South Asia through the Harappan Period. In S. Settar and R. Korisettar (eds), *Protohistory: Archaeology of the Harappan Civilization*, 391-408. Indian Archaeology in Retrospect. vol. II. New Delhi, Indian Council of Historical Research and Manohar.

Meena, B. R. and A. Tripathi. 2001. Further excavation at Ojiyana. *Puratattva* 31, 73-77.

Meena, B. R. and A. Tripathi. 2001-2002. Excavations at Ojiyana: A unique copper age site in Aravalli. *Pragdhara* 12, 45-66.

Mishra, A. R. 2000. *Chalcolithic Ceramics of Balathal, District Udaipur, Rajasthan*. Unpublished Ph.D. Dissertation. Deccan College.

Misra, V. N. 1967. *Pre- and Proto-History of the Berach Basin South Rajasthan*. Pune, Deccan College Postgraduate and Research Institute.

Misra, V. N. 1971a. Two late Mesolithic settlements in Rajasthan—a brief review of investigations. *Poona University Journal (Humanities)* 35, 59-77.

Misra, V. N. 1971b. Two microlithic sites in Rajasthan—a preliminary investigation. *The Eastern Anthropologist* 24(3), 237-88.

Misra, V. N. 1973. Bagor: a late Mesolithic settlement in north-west India. *World Archaeology* 5(1), 92-100.

Misra, V. N. 1982. Bagor: the archaeological setting. In J. R. Lukacs, V. N. Misra and K. A. R. Kennedy (eds), *Bagor and Tilwara: Late Mesolithic Cultures of Northwest India, Volume I: The Human Skeletal Remains*, 9-20. Pune, Deccan College Postgraduate and Research Institute.

Misra, V. N., V. Shinde, R. K. Mohanty, K. Dalal, A. Mishra, L. Pandey and J. Kharakwal. 1995. The excavations at Balathal: Their contribution to the Chalcolithic and Iron Age cultures of Mewar. *Man and Environment* 20(1), 57-80.

Misra, V. N., V. Shinde, R. K. Mohanty and L. Pandey. 1993. Terracotta bull figurines from Marmi: A Chalcolithic settlement in Chitorgarh District, Rajasthan. *Man and Environment* 18(2), 149-152.

Misra, V. N., V. Shinde, R. K. Mohanty, L. Pandey and J. Kharakwal. 1997. Excavations at Balathal, Udaipur District, Rajasthan (1995-97), with special reference to Chalcolithic architecture. *Man and Environment* 22(2), 35-60.

Mittra, S. K. and V. Shivananda. 2000. Chalcolithic settlements at Chichali. *Puratattva* 30, 45-49.

Mohanty, R. K., A. Mishra, P. Joglekar, P. K. Thomas, J. Kharakwal and T. Panda. 2000. Purani Marmi: A late Ahar Culture settlement in Chittaurgarh District, Rajasthan. *Puratattva* 30, 132-141.

Pandey, S. K. 1982. Chalcolithic Eran and its Chronology. In R. K. Sharma (ed.), *Indian Archaeology: New Perspectives*, 249-56. Delhi, Agam Kala Prakashan.

Possehl, G. L. 2002. Harappans and hunters: Economic interaction and specialization in prehistoric India. In K. D. Morrison and L. Junker (eds), *Forager-Traders in South and Southeast Asia: Long term histories*, 62-76. Cambridge, Cambridge University Press.

Possehl, G. L. and K. A. R. Kennedy. 1979. Hunter-gatherer/agriculturalist exchange in prehistory: an Indian example. *Current Anthropology* 20(3), 592-93.

Possehl, G. L. and P. C. Rissman. 1992. The chronology of prehistoric India: From earliest times to the Iron Age. In R. W. Ehrich (ed.), *Chronologies in Old World Archaeology*, 465-90 and 447-74. 3rd edition. Chicago, University of Chicago Press.

Raczek, T. P. 2007. *Shared Histories: Technology and Community at Gilund and Bagor, Rajasthan, India (c. 3000-1700 BC)*, Unpublished Ph.D. Dissertation. University of Pennsylvania.

Raczek, T. P. 2010. In the context of copper: Indian lithics in the third millennium BC. In B. V. Eriksen (ed.), *Lithic Technology in Metal Using Societies*, 231-45. Proceedings of a UISPP Workshop, Lisbon, September 2006. Højbjerg: Jutland Archaeological Society.

Sankalia, H. D. 1969. Pottery introduction. In H. D. Sankalia, S. B. Deo and Z. D. Ansari (eds), *Excavations at Ahar (Tambavati)*, 18-28. Pune, Deccan College.

Sankalia, H. D. 1979. *Prehistory and Protohistory of India and Pakistan*. Pune, Deccan College.

Sankalia, H. D., S. B. Deo and Z. D. Ansari. 1969. *Excavations at Ahar (Tambavati)*. Pune, Deccan College Post-graduate and Research Institute.

Sankalia, H. D., S. B. Deo and Z. D. Ansari. 1971. Chalcolithic Navdatoli *Chalcolithic Navdatoli: The excavations at Navdatoli 1957-59*. Publication No. 2. Pune/Baroda, Deccan College Postgraduate and Research Institute/Maharaja Sayajiro University.

Sankalia, H. D., B. Subbarao and S. B. Deo. 1958. *The Excavations at Maheshwar and Navdatoli 1952-53*. Poona/Baroda, Deccan College Post-graduate and Research Institute.

Shah, D. R. 1969. Animal remains from excavations at Ahar. In H. D. Sankalia, S. B. Deo and Z. D. Ansari (eds), *Excavations at Ahar (Timbavati)*, 237-245. Pune, Deccan College Post-graduate and Research Institute.

Shinde, V. and G. L. Possehl. 2005. A report on the excavations at Gilund, 1999-2001. In C. Jarrige and V. Lefèvre (eds), *South Asian Archaeology 2001*, 293-302. Paris, Éditions Recherche sur les Civilisations.

Shinde, V., G. L. Possehl and M. Ameri. 2005. Excavations at Gilund 2001-2003: The seal impressions and other finds. In U. Franke-Vogt and H.-J. Weisshaar (eds), *South Asian Archaeology 2003*, 159-169. Aachen, Linden Soft.

Shinde, V., G. L. Possehl and S. S. Deshpande. 2002. The ceramic assemblage in proto-historic Mewar (Rajasthan), with special reference to Gilund and Balathal. *Puratattva* (32), 5-24.

Thomas, P. K. 1975. The role of animals in the food economy of the Mesolithic culture of Western and Central India. In A. T. Clason (ed.), *Archaeozoological Studies*, 322-28. Amsterdam, North-Holland.

Thomas, P. K. 1977. *Archaeozoological Aspects of the Prehistoric Cultures of Western India*. Unpublished Ph.D. Dissertation. Pune, Deccan College.

Thomas, P. K. 1984. The faunal background of the Chalcolithic culture of western India. In J. Clutton-Brock and C. Greigson (eds), *Animals and Archaeology: 3. Early Herders and Their Flocks*, 355-62. International Series, 202. Oxford, British Archaeological Reports.

Thomas, P. K. and P. P. Joglekar. 1996. Faunal remains from Balathal: A preliminary report. *Man and Environment* 21(1), 91-97.

Vishnu-Mittre. 1969. Remains of rice and millet. In H. D. Sankalia, S. B. Deo and Z. D. Ansari (eds), *Excavations at Ahar (Timbavati)*, 229-236. Pune, Deccan College Post-graduate and Research Institute.

Wakankar, V. S. 1969. Kayatha excavation. *Ujjain, Vikram University Journal, Special Number*.

2. Development from Mesolithic to Chalcolithic in the Mewar Region of Rajasthan: Contribution of Gilund Excavation

Vasant Shinde

Introduction

Excavations at the sites of Ahar, Bagor, Balathal, Marmi, and Ojiyana have added immensely to the understanding of cultural processes and long distance contact from fifth to the second millennia BC in the Mewar region of Rajasthan. Recent excavations at the site of Gilund demonstrate that it also has much to contribute to the archaeology of the region. Most importantly, the excavations at Gilund revealed evidence of a very early occupation that shows continuous occupation from the Mesolithic to the Chalcolithic. This evidence contradicts suggestions that the Chalcolithic culture in Mewar results from migrations and requires an explanation for the causes of cultural development from the Mesolithic to the Early and Mature Chalcolithic.

The Mewar region of Rajasthan is no doubt one of the most fertile regions of India, adjoining the fertile Chambal Basin, the Malwa Plateau and the North Gujarat region that is rich in pastureland. In addition to agricultural and pastoral abundance, plentiful minerals and metals can be found in the Aravallis, which surround the Mewar region on the west and north. The archaeology of this region has been investigated through exploration and excavation for over 50 years. V.N. Misra's exploration of the Banas/Berach Basin in the late 1950s (1967) was most rewarding as he discovered many sites of different cultural periods, particularly the Protohistoric period. The first archaeological site to be subjected to full excavations was that of Ahar, on the outskirts then, but now in the heart of the city of Udaipur, in the late 1950s and early 1960s. The excavation carried out by Deccan College under the direction of Prof. H. D. Sankalia (Sankalia *et al.*, 1969) provided a nearly complete cultural sequence from the Chalcolithic to the Medieval periods for the Mewar region. After the excavations at Ahar, little significant archaeological research was conducted until 1993, when the site of Balathal was selected for large-scale excavations (Misra *et al.*, 1997, Shinde, 2000). Subsequently, the sites of Gilund in Rajsamand District (Possehl *et al.*, 2004; Shinde 2002; Shinde and Possehl, 2005; Shinde *et al.*, 2005) and Ojiyana in Bhilwara District (Meena and Tripathi 2000; 2001; 2001-02) were also fully excavated. Based on these excavations and related fresh research a number of Master's dissertations (Hanlon 2006, Kashyap 1997; Sinha 1998, Dibyopama 2006) and Ph.D. dissertations (Dasgupta 2005, Mishra 2000, Sinha 2003, Raczek 2007, Boivin 2001 and Ameri 2010) have been produced, and a few more are currently in progress. Thus, since the 1990s this region has witnessed a quantum jump in archaeological research activities.

One of the most important contributions of the excavations at Gilund is the discovery of the Mesolithic phase and the cultural transition from hunting-gathering to agriculture in the Mewar region. This significant pioneer research has enabled the identification of Mewar as yet another primary zone in the subcontinent for the origins of village life and possibly domestication, the first being in and around Mehrgarh in Baluchistan hills. The favourable climatic conditions, good arable land, availability of natural resources, as well as trade relations with Harappans and other contemporary Chalcolithic communities in the adjoining region, appear to have been responsible for a sedentary life and cultural development in this region. Excavations at Balathal and Gilund have enabled the reconstruction of various technologies that were in use between 3700-1500 BC in the Mewar region of Rajasthan. With the shift to agriculture from hunting-gathering, there was a change in the structure from the kind of social organization that characterised the earlier egalitarian, band-level hunting-gathering community. Studies carried out on the social-economic aspect by scholars as Shinde (1991), Dhavalikar *et al.*, (1988), and Sinha (1998) have already demonstrated this change with actual archaeological evidence.

The large number of Palaeolithic and Mesolithic sites in southeast Rajasthan testifies to the existence of hunting-gathering communities in the region. The changing environment, population pressure and depleting resources led the Mesolithic hunters to adopt an agrarian lifestyle. Small settlements with an agro-pastoral economy along with hunting and gathering developed in areas such as the area surrounding Balathal. The beginning was modest, but with increasing prosperity and surplus, various crafts were developed including ceramics, permanent structures, and copper technology. The need for living space led to the development of new settlements and exchange networks between them (such as between Ahar, Balathal and Gilund) that facilitated the procurement of non-local goods in exchange for locally produced products. At Balathal and Gilund large silos, storage bins mud platforms and structures identified as possible granaries give us a clear indication of the strong agricultural base in the economy. Faunal analysis reveals the predominance of cattle, followed by sheep and goats and supplemented by wild animals and fish. With this shift in subsistence and the development of sedentary settlements, a marked change in social organization occurred as cultural requirements entailed adaptation to economic and ecological environments and needs. Increasing need for co-operation and organization of activities relating to subsistence led to a division of labour. More efficiency and surpluses required administrative mechanisms for storage, allocation and redistribution. Authority also played an important role in the administration of pastures, water sources and all other collectively held and produced goods. Surpluses allowed more time and the ability to support skilled and specialised crafts not possessed by all members of the society thus enhancing trade and exchange. These socio-economic changes led to the development of a chiefdom type society for restructuring and administering these changes. In addition, there seems to have existed a relation between the Harappans of Gujarat and Rajasthan at the time. It is argued that trade with the Harappans was responsible for these communities attaining a status of incipient urbanization in this region (Shinde 2000; Shinde et al., 2004).

Based on the detailed observation of surrounding ecological conditions and the nature of sites, a hierarchy of settlements has been reconstructed. The sites range in size from 0.3 hectares (Tarawat), to 22 hectares (Gilund), but many fall in the five-hectare range. The site of Gilund appears to have been the regional centre of the Ahar Culture because of its strategic location in the centre of the Basin and because of its size. In addition, many settlements of medium size located in the proximity of fertile arable land have been identified as farming settlements, while settlements like Ahar at the foot of the Aravalli Hills near copper ore deposits probably specialised in copper working.

Extensive and intensive excavations carried out over different parts of the site of Gilund aimed at elaborating on the archaeological narrative established thus far.

The Beginning Phase

Based on the data provided by the first systematic excavations carried out at the site of Ahar in the late 1950s and early 1960s, it was thought that the beginning of settled life in this region went back to the last quarter of the third millennium BC and that the people migrated here with the advanced technology from elsewhere. The Harappans were projected as the major source of inspiration for the development of agricultural communities in this part (Dhavalikar 1979). However, the evidence from the excavations at Balathal convincingly demonstrated that there was an indigenous development of village life, which goes back to the middle of the fourth millennium BC, much before the development of the Harappan Civilization. The development is thought to be gradual, as seen in the material culture, particularly in structures and pottery. This gradual cultural process culminated into the formation of a flourishing and developed phase around the middle of third millennium BC. The first farmers lived in small circular or rectangular houses and manufactured coarse pottery. One of the most important features of the pottery is the production of Reserve-Slipped ware. The presence of a large amount of this pottery, coupled with scientific analysis (Gogte 1996) clearly suggests its indigenous production. Most of the wares of the Chalcolithic Ahar culture such as Black-and-Red ware, Thin Red-Slipped, and Tan Ware were introduced in the early phase. In addition, the presence of a few copper tools suggests the development of this technique along with the origins of the settlement. There is a possibility that the art of extracting copper from ore was known throughout the region, as the studies carried out by Arunima Kashyap on the lithic tools from Bagor, suggests the possibility of the employment of copper punches for stone blade production at that site. That this technology was definitely carried forward in the Chalcolithic without change is demonstrated at Inamgaon (Shinde 1988). They also manufactured a variety of food processing equipments such as saddle querns, rubber stones, mullers, etc. The presence of the underground storage silos and food processing equipment in the Early Chalcolithic period demonstrates the importance of agriculture in the life of the Chalcolithic people throughout all phases. This is the picture emerging from the lower levels at both Balathal and Gilund.

The site of Gilund has provided additional evidence compared to the site of Balathal. The earliest occupation at Balathal lies directly the bedrock. However, at Gilund, there is a Mesolithic settlement, dated to the late sixth and early fifth millennium BC, located below the Chalcolithic occupation, and resting on a sand dune. This is very important, as there is clear indication of the transformation from the Mesolithic to Chalcolithic at the site. This is the first site in India where such evidence has been encountered. These Mesolithic people cleared vegetation and grass on the site and burned it before establishing a settlement on the ancient sand dune. This is evident from a thin burned layer found at the base of the Mesolithic settlement at Gilund, which was possibly formed by such a burning. In addition, the presence of floors and traces of huts are indicative of the permanent nature of settlement. The discovery of food processing equipment suggests subsistence based on agriculture.

The most systematic and scientific work done on the Bagor material indicates gradual change from Aceramic to Ceramic Mesolithic phases at Bagor (Shinde et al., 2004). The results of the floral material collected are not yet available. However, Arunima Kashyap from Michigan State University, USA has just completed her research for her Ph.D. dissertation on the use wear and starch grain analysis on the Bagor lithics which provides great insight into subsistence strategies used at the site. The following quotations from her Ph.D. dissertation summarise her finds (2006):

> The analysis reveals the various activities such as hide working (25% of used tools), meat and fish processing (12% of used tools), woodworking (9 % of used tools) and plant cutting (15% of used tools) were carried out at the site during the Aceramic phase. During the Ceramic Mesolithic Phase at Bagor the prehistoric people participated in activities such as hide work (20% of used tools), meat and fish processing (9% of used tools), wood work (17% of used tools) and plant cutting (36% of used tools). (Kashyap 2006, 125).

In addition, a decrease from of tools used for hunting from the Aceramic to the Ceramic Phases (15% to 6%) 'suggests that there was a significant change in the subsistence activities at the site during the Ceramic phase.' (2006, 211). Kashyap's starch grain analysis found that:

> Aceramic inhabitants of Bagor were subsisting on a mixed economy. They exploited root crops possibly *Zingiber* (Ginger) and *Cyperus*, vegetables possibly *Solanaum* (Eggplant), grasses like *Sesamum* (Sesame), beans/pulses like *Macrotyloma* (Horse gram) and fruits possibly *Phoenix* (Date Palm) and *Mangifera* (Mango). New plants are added to the economy during the Ceramic phase: including fruits, possibly *Tamarindus* (Tamarind), *Phoenix* (Date Palm) and *Mangifera* (Mango). Beans/pulses like Vigna species and possibly *Cajanus* (Pigeon pea) are added to the list with *Macrotyloma* (Horse gram). Although more research with both introduced and local millets in India needs to be done before anything can be securely said about the finds of millets, there is evidence of the introduction of new species probably domesticated in Africa including possibly Eleusine (Finger Millets) and Sorghum (Jowar) at Bagor during the Ceramic phase. Also interesting is the starch grain: possibly Hordeum (Barley) on the grinder studied from the Ceramic phase at Bagor. (Kashyap 2006, 218).

"Kashyap's" finds are very interesting because this would indicate agriculture 'on the Indian subcontinent may have included several levels of "man-plant relationship," from acquaintance through excessive exploitation to cultivation of indigenous seed crops which were subsequently transformed by the introduction of higher yielding crops like wheat and barley, introduced from South-West Asia.' (2006, 205). In her final analysis which supports the finds of Shinde *et al.*, 2004, Kashyap proposes that,

> improved climatic conditions (around 10,000 years ago) and abundance of plants and animal food in the semi arid region of Western India led to an explosion of hunter-gatherer populations here (Misra and Rajguru 1989; Shinde *et al.*, 2004). Changing environment around the middle of the Holocene, population pressure and depleting resources, however, all forced these hunter-gatherer groups to settle in congenial environments that had better resources, such as water and plant (provided opportunities for selecting local cultigens) and animal life (Shinde 2002; Shinde *et al.*, 2004). (Kashyap 2006, 226-7).

The explosion of hunter-gatherer populations is also evident in the increase in the number of Mesolithic settlements in Rajasthan, Malwa and Gujarat except Kutch (Shinde *et al.*, 2004). The subsistence pattern developed in the later part of the Mesolithic phase continued into the early Chalcolithic.

The most significant discovery in the Mesolithic phase is that of the ceramic assemblage which dates to 5000 BC and represents the earliest ceramics in this part of the country. Two wares, namely Coarse Red and Grey, have been found. Both of them are handmade from coarse clay; the former is sometimes decorated with simple geometric incised linear patterns. Unfortunately, as the pottery is very brittle, it has only survived in small fragments and the shapes cannot be reconstructed. Both of these wares continued into the Early Chalcolithic phase with some modification. This is one of the best pieces of evidence of the transition from the Mesolithic to Chalcolithic at the site. The other evidence in this respect comes in the form of structures. In the Mesolithic levels, the floors of circular huts were made of alternate layers of fine sand and silt and rammed hard. Significantly, similar evidence is reported from the Early Chalcolithic at Balathal, which is yet another important sign of the transformation (Shinde 2000). There is of course continuation of the lithic stone tool tradition from the Mesolithic to Chalcolithic at the site of Gilund (Raczek 2007). The above evidence is a clear indication of the Mesolithic transformation from a hunting-gathering, incipient agriculture stage to a fully settled way of life in this region. As this is outside of Baluchistan (which holds the sites Mehrgarh and Kile Ghul Mohammad) it confirms the presence of a second primary zone of development of agriculture and agricultural communities. This is another region that can be identified as giving birth to the origins of agriculture and settled way of life in the later half of the fourth millennium BC. The data from the lower levels at Gilund and Balathal is scant as excavations in the lower levels were very limited; therefore it is not possible to generalise the conclusions. This is the beginning of the discovery of such evidence and there is a greater need to generate ample data to draw meaningful conclusions.

Developed Phase

The developed phase shows many signs of prosperity and growth, resulting in population growth and territorial expansion. The entire Banas-Berach Basin came under occupation as a result of prosperity and population growth. In addition, settlements extended into the parts of the Chambal Basin and Malwa Plateau. As these settlements were located in different ecological zones such the Chambal Valley and Malwa Plateau, the growing population may have been ensured a steady supply of food. Based on the series of dates obtained from Balathal, this developed phase of the Chalcolithic can be dated between 2500-2000 BC.

The excavations at Gilund and Balathal have demonstrated a gradual development and prosperity in the material culture of the Chalcolithic people from 2900 BC; by 2500 BC there was a drastic change in the life-style of the people. Extensive evidence of the structural remains of the Mature phase has been excavated at both Gilund and Balathal. Some of the noticeable changes observed in the structural activities of this phase include: 1. use of mud-bricks and burnt bricks on a large scale for construction, 2. introduction of a modicum of planning, 3. establishment of craft manufacturing and storage facilities within the settlements, 4. emergence of public architecture, and 5. establishment of long distance trade and contacts.

All the structures excavated in the Middle Chalcolithic are made either of mud-bricks or burnt bricks. The use of burnt brick was identified in the structures exposed on the southern part of GLD- 2, which also has evidence of craft manufacture. It was observed that only the structures identified as manufacturing units on this part of the mound were made of burnt bricks. All other structures including domestic and public were otherwise made of mud bricks. There is an identical picture at Balathal. However, as stone is commonly available around the site of Balathal, it was the principal building material throughout the Chalcolithic period at that site. In the case of Gilund, building stone is not available in large quantity. Instead, they used bricks on a large scale as there is very fine quality clay available near the site, which was exploited by the Chalcolithic people. Even today, one can notice a flourishing brick-making industry in the area around the modern Gilund village (Dasgupta 2005).

Though several houses were excavated at Gilund, they were not horizontally exposed and therefore it is not possible to make definitive statements about the planning of those structures. In general, though, the structures are large and very well made. In addition, a number of large complexes came into existence. It is possible that a modicum of planning was adopted at Gilund. In contrast to Gilund, Balathal was horizontally excavated in an extensive area. This enabled the archaeologists to identify a planned settlement consisting of a main street, lanes and structures arranged on both sides. This evidence indicates the development of urbanization in the Mewar region contemporary to the Harappans.

One conspicuous feature at Gilund was the presence of a large number of storage pits, both small and big, very well made and either plastered with lime or lined with grass. Also there is a large, possibly public granary/storage made of parallel mud-brick walls. This evidence indicates that the site of Gilund was a major grain-producing Chalcolithic village and that the subsistence of the inhabitants was based on agriculture. Being located in the centre of the Banas Basin and large in size, it can even be identified as a regional centre. Even today, Gilund is a prosperous agricultural village in the area and the main occupation of the people in the village is farming. Extensive and intensive farming is possible because of the presence of very fertile arable land and the availability of a good supply of water. The discovery of a number of farmsteads in the catchment area of Gilund further underlines the importance of agricultural activities during the Chalcolithic and even Early Historic periods (Dasgupta 2005). If the views of Gurdeep Singh and others (1974) are accepted, the climate between 3000 and 2000 BC was wetter than today, and it therefore can be presumed that the River Banas was possibly a perennial river and carried more water at that time than in recent years. In addition, there are a couple of lakes in the vicinity of the ancient site, which may have existed in the Chalcolithic. The river and lakes both may have provided a source of water for domestic use as well as for field irrigation.

The presence of a large number of artefacts in the Middle Chalcolithic level is an indication of the prosperity and flourishing of manufacturing activity at the site. The discovery of finished and unfinished objects, tools that were employed in the manufacturing activities and workshops further confirm the presence of craft manufacture. There is no direct evidence that the pottery was manufactured at the site. However, considering the quantity of the pottery found in the excavation and the size of the settlement, it can safely be presumed that the majority of pottery was manufactured there. In addition, the discovery of dabbers (used mainly in shaping pots) and some vitrified potsherds (indicators of local pottery-firing) are testimony to the manufacturing of pottery onsite. As a rectangular closed kiln for firing fine wares was discovered in the same phase at the site of Balathal (Shinde 2000), it is expected that similar kilns may have existed at the site of Gilund as well.

The various ceramic assemblages such as Black-and-Red ware, Thin Red-Slipped, Tan ware, Coarse Red and Grey wares found at the site in the Middle Chalcolithic levels were almost entirely wheel-made and very well fired. They surely evolved from the Early Chalcolithic levels which demonstrates an advancement in technology over the previous phase. A large number of terracotta bull figurines found at Gilund, may or may not have been manufactured at the site. The site of Marmi, 20 km to the northeast of Gilund, where hundreds of terracotta bull figurines have been found on the surface, has been identified as bull figuring manufacture place (Misra et al., 1993). Considering its proximity to Gilund there is a scope to presume that the bull figurines at Gilund may have come from Marmi. The presence of copper objects in the Chalcolithic phase is not great, but copper objects are found throughout the Chalcolithic phase. They occur in large numbers in the Middle phase, showing prosperity, but no change in technology has been identified. It has been demonstrated that the copper tool assemblages were locally manufactured by cold-hammer technology at Balathal (Srivastav et al., 2003) and the same is presumably true for Gilund as well. In addition, important sites like Ahar, Balathal and Gilund have evidence of copper tool production in the form of furnaces. The evidence found at Gilund is much larger compared with the other two sites. On the southern end of the GLD-2 the remains of a large copper furnace with a large amount of slag was excavated. The furnace, large and oval in shape, is located in a structure. Most of the structures excavated on this part of GLD-2 appear to have been associated with the manufacturing activities.

There are a number of reasons for the development of the Chalcolithic phase in the Mewar region. Of course, the climate may have played an important role as is indicated by some scholars (Singh 1971). However, on the basis of the evidence from the sites of Gilund and Balathal, one of the important factors responsible for their development was trade contacts with the Harappans. The Harappans and Chalcolithic people of Mewar developed contacts with each other around 2500 BC, resulting in reciprocal cultural impact and exchange.

Three main pieces of evidence connect the Harappans and the Chalcolithic people of Mewar: pottery, copper manufacture, and architecture. First, it appears that the Harappans may have adopted the technique and tradition of the Reserve Slipped ware from the Chalcolithic. This particular pottery was introduced and manufactured first by the Chalcolithic community of Mewar sometime towards the end of fourth millennium BC. The presence of a few Reserve Slipped ware sherds at a few Harappan sites were thought to have come from the west mainly because of the contacts. However, the possible source of this tradition can now be traced to the Early Chalcolithic period in the Mewar region. In addition, the Tan ware found in this phase at Gilund and Balathal resembles the Harappan Red ware in terms of technique of manufacture, fabric, firing and vessel forms. Its absence in the Early levels and sudden appearance in the Mature level, leads to this hypothesis.

It is not unlikely that the Harappans were supplied food grains and copper (most probably finished tools as similar tools have been reported from the Chalcolithic levels here) by the Chalcolithic people of Mewar. As far as copper sources are concerned, it is argued that the source of raw material is available in the Aravalli mountain ranges, which are close to the Chalcolithic settlements. Objects found in Harappan as well as Chalcolithic levels were made by the cold hammering technique. Numerous objects such as razor blades, knives, chisels, arrowheads, etc. recovered from this phase are typologically similar to those found in the Harappan levels. The contact with the Harappans enabled the Chalcolithic people to import shell and shell objects, marine gastropods, fish, semi-precious stones or objects made thereof from the Harappan region, particularly Saurashtra. The trade route may have run through North Gujarat, where a number of Harappan sites along with typical Ahar Black-and-Red ware pottery, have been reported. This evidence indicates movement in this region of the Chalcolithic Mewar and Harappan tradition.

Finally, the massive use of mud-bricks for construction and the sudden introduction of the header and stretcher method of construction in the Middle Chalcolithic level are attributed to the Harappan impact. Only the Harappan people were aware of the use of burnt bricks and this construction method which was borrowed by the Chalcolithic people after establishing contacts. The discovery at Balathal of a sudden emergence, without any precedence, of a well planned settlement with multi-roomed building complexes on either side of a street, exactly similar to those uncovered at the Harappan sites of Kuntasi, Rojdi, etc in Saurashtra, most probably reflects Harappan impact. It was observed at Balathal that the walls of the outer fortification and the fortified enclosure were broad at the base and slightly tapered upwards, similar to the method followed by the Harappans in their cities and towns.

The sudden prosperity around 2500 BC in the Mewar region could have triggered a population explosion. The entire Banas/Berach Basin was densely occupied as the discovery of more than 110 settlements so far indicates. In addition, the Chalcolithic people of Mewar (Ahar culture) extended their settlements in Central India, up to Navdatoli in the Malwa Plateau. The presence of a chief in the society, the division of labour, strong hinterland trade and emergence of a craft specialization prompted fast and steady progress of the Chalcolithic community in Mewar. These factors led the Chalcolithic phase in the Mewar region to the threshold of urbanization.

Bibliography

Ameri, M. 2010. *Sealing at the Edge of the Middle Asian Interaction Sphere: The View from Gilund, Rajasthan, India.* Unpublished Ph.D. Dissertation. Institute of Fine Arts, New York University.

Boivin, N. 2001. *'Archaeological Science as Anthropology': Space, Time and Materiality in Rural India and the Ancient Past.* Unpublished Ph.D. Thesis, University of Cambridge.

Dasgupta, D. 2005. *Site Catchment Analysis of the Chalcolithic site of Gilund, Rajsamand District, Mewar.* Unpublished Ph.D. Dissertation, Deccan College.

Dhavalikar, M. K. 1979. Chalcolithic cultures of Central India. In D. P. Agrawal and D. K. Chakarabarti (eds), *Essays in Indian Protohistory*, 229-45. New Delhi, B. R. Publishing Corporation.

Dhavalikar, M. K., H. D. Sankalia and Z. D. Ansari, 1988. *Excavations at Inamgaon*, vol I, parts-i- ii, Pune, Deccan College Research Institute.

Dibyopama, A. 2006. *Site Catchment Analysis of Balathal.* Unpublished M. A. Dissertation. Deccan College.

Gogte, V. D. 1996. Chalcolithic Balathal—A trading center as revealed by the XRD study of ancient pottery. *Man and Environment* 21(1), 103-110.

Hanlon, J. A. 2006. *The Gilund Terracottas: A New Look at the Ahar Culture in Rajasthan and Madhya Pradesh.* Unpublished M.Phil. Thesis. University of Cambridge.

Kashyap, A. 1999. *Harappan Impact on the Chalcolithic Culture of Central India.* Unpublished M. A. Dissertation. Deccan College.

Kashyap, A. 2006. *Use-wear and starch-grain analysis: An integrated approach to understanding the transition from hunting gathering to food production at Bagor, Rajasthan, India.* Unpublished Ph.D. Dissertation, Michigan State University.

Meena, B. R. and Tripathi, A. 2000. Excavation at Ojiyana. *Puratattva* 30, 67-73.

Meena, B. R. and Tripathi, A. 2001. Further Excavation at Ojiyana. *Puratattva* 31, 73-77.

Meena, B. R. and Tripathi, A. 2001-2002. Excavations at Ojiyana: An Unique Copper Age Site in Aravalli. *Pragdhara* 12, 45-66.

Mishra, A. R. 2000. *Chalcolithic Ceramics of Balathal, District Udaipur, Rajasthan*. Unpublished Ph.D. Disseration. Deccan College.

Misra, V. N. 1967. *Pre-and Proto-history of the Berach Basin, South Rajasthan*. Pune, Deccan College Research Institute.

Misra, V. N. and S. N. Rajguru. 1989. Palaeoenvironment and prehistory of the Thar Desert, Rajasthan, India. In K. Frifelt and P. Sorensen (eds), South Asian Archaeology 1985, 296-320. London, Curzon Press.

Misra, V. N., V. Shinde, R. K. Mohanty and L. Pandey. 1993. Terra-cotta bull figurines from Marmi: A Chalcolithic settlement in Chitorgarh District, Rajasthan, *Man and Environment*, 18(2), 149-152.

Misra, V. N., V. Shinde, R. K. Mohanty, L. Pandey and J. Kharakwal. 1997. Excavations at Balathal, Udaipur District, Rajasthan (1995-97), with Special Reference to Chalcolithic Architecture, *Man and Environment* 22 (2), 35-59.

Possehl. G. L., V. Shinde and M. Ameri, 2004; The Ahar-Banas Complex and the BMAC, *Man and Environment*, 30 (2), 10-29.

Raczek, T. P. 2007. *Shared Histories: Technology and Community at Gilund and Bagor, Rajasthan, India (c. 3000-1700 BC)*. Unpublished Ph. D. Dissertation. University of Pennsylvania.

Sankalia, H. D., S. B. Deo and Z. D.Ansari. 1969. *Excavations at Ahar (Timbavati)*. Pune, Deccan College.

Shinde, V., 1988. A note on copper punch. In M. K. Dhavalikar, H. D. Sankalia and Z. D. Ansari (eds), *Excavations at Inamgaon*, vol. I, part ii, 725-726. Pune, Deccan College Research Institute.

Shinde, V. 1991. Craft specialization and social organization in the Chalcolithic Deccan, India. *Antiquity* 65(249), 796-807.

Shinde, V. 2000. The origin and development of the Chalcolithic in Central India. In *Indo Pacific Prehistory Association Bulletin* 19, 125-36.

Shinde, V. 2002. Emergence, development and spread of agricultural communities in South Asia. In Y. Yasuda (ed.), *Origins of Pottery and Agriculture*, Singapore, Roli Books and Lustre Press.

Shinde, V. and G. L. Possehl 2005. A report on the excavations at Gilund, 1999-2001. In C. Jarrige and V. Lefèvre (eds), *South Asian Archaeology 2001: Proceedings of the Sixteenth International Conference of the European Association of South Asian Archaeologists*, 293-309. Vol. 1 Prehistory. Paris, Éditions Recherche sur les Civilisations.

Shinde, V., G. L. Possehl and M. Ameri. 2005. Excavations at Gilund 2001-2003: The seal impressions and other finds. In U. Franke-Vogt and H.-J. Weisshaar (eds), *South Asian Archaeology 2003*, 159-169. Aachen, Linden Soft.

Shinde, V., S. Sinha Deshpande and Y. Yasuda. 2004. Human response to Holocene climate changes: A case study of Western India between 5th to 3rd millennium BC. In Y. Yasuda and V. Shinde (eds), *Monsoon and Civilization,* 383-406. Singapore, Roli Books and Lustre Press.

Singh, G. 1971. The Indus Valley culture seen in context of post-glacial climatic and ecological studies in north-west India. *Archaeology and Physical Anthropology in Oceania*, 6(2), 177-189.

Singh, G., R. D. Joshi, S. K. Chopra and A. B. Singh. 1974. Late Quaternary history of vegetation and climate of the Rajasthan Desert, India. *Philosophical Transactions of the Royal Society of London* 267, 467-501.

Sinha, S. 1998. *Study of Chalcolithic Social Organization in Central India with Special Reference to Balathal*. Unpublished M. A. Dissertation. Pune, Deccan College.

Sinha, S. D. 2003. *A study of Cultural Interactions in Western India in the 3rd and 2nd Millennium BC*. Unpublished Ph. D. Thesis. Deccan College.

Srivastav, A., R. Balasubrmaniam and V. N. Misra. 2003. Metallurgical investigations on a Chalcolithic copper nail from Balathal. *Man and Environment* 28(1), 33-40.

3. An Overview of the Antiquities from the 1999-2005 Excavations at Gilund, a Chalcolithic Site in Southeast Rajasthan

Julie A. Hanlon

Excavations at Gilund were conducted under the direction of Dr. Gregory Possehl of the University of Pennsylvania and Dr. Vasant Shinde of the Deccan College, Pune. As an undergraduate I became involved with this project in 2002 and excavated during two of the five field seasons. From September 2004 to May 2005, I was given the opportunity to organise, document and curate the antiquities from all five field seasons. This paper will present a brief overview of the kinds of materials recovered there and how these materials link Gilund with other excavated Ahar-Banas sites in Rajasthan.

The Ahar-Banas is one of several Chalcolithic cultures which emerged in northwest India in the third millennium BC. The range in chronology is 3200 to 1400 BC, although dates at Balathal begin c. 3700 BC or earlier (Misra 2005). The majority of sites are concentrated in the river valleys of southeast Rajasthan, and there are also a number of sites with Ahar-Banas material culture in eastern Madhya Pradesh.

The most distinctive feature of the Ahar-Banas is the white-painted Black-and-Red ware. It is primarily the presence and concentration of this diagnostic ware, identified during surface explorations, which has been used to classify Ahar-Banas sites. By examining the antiquities uncovered at Gilund, I hope to demonstrate that the Ahar-Banas sites share related cultural assemblages, which go beyond their diagnostic white-painted Black-and-Red ware. Striking similarities appear between the antiquities found at Gilund and those from other Ahar-Banas sites in Rajasthan.

Excavated Ahar-Banas Sites in Rajasthan

The five excavated sites of the Ahar-Banas in Rajasthan are Ahar, Balathal, Gilund, Purani Marmi and Ojiyana. The locations and chronologies for these sites are presented in Figure 3.1. Ahar is the type site of the Ahar-Banas cultural complex and was first excavated by R. C. Agrawal in the 1950s (IAR 1955, 1956), and later from 1961-2 by a team from Deccan College, Pune (IAR 1962). Ahar consists of a single large mound, now dissected by a modern road, and is situated within the modern city of Udaipur, close to the Ahar River. The 1961-2 excavations were published by H. D. Sankalia and colleagues from Deccan College in 1969 (Sankalia *et al.*, 1969). Because Ahar is currently the only Ahar-Banas site in Rajasthan with a fully published site report, this volume exerts considerable influence on how we conceptualise the Ahar-Banas. The future publication of site reports from other Ahar-Banas and contemporary sites in Rajasthan will help to broaden our understanding of this culture and its regional significance.

SITE	LOCATION	CHRONOLOGY	
Ahar	Udaipur district (24° 35′ N, 73° 44′ E)	Period Ia Period Ib Period Ic Period II Early Historic	2600-2150 BC 2150-1950 BC 1950-1500 BC
		Coordinates from Hooja (1988)	
		Chronology from Possehl and Rissman (1992)	
Balathal	Udaipur district (24° 43′ N, 73° 59′ E)	Phase A Phase B Early Historic	3700-2500 BC 2500-1600 BC
		Coordinates from Misra *et al.* (1997)	
		Chronology from Misra (2005)	
Gilund	Rajsamand district (25° 01′ 56″ N, 74° 15′ 45″ E)	Middle Chalcolithic Late Chalcolithic Early Historic	2500-2000 BC 2000-1700 BC
		Coordinates from Shinde and Possehl (2005)	
		Chronology from Shinde *et al.* (2005)	
Ojiyana	Bhilwara district (25° 53′ N, 74° 21′ E)	Phase I Phase II Phase III	3000-2500 BC 2500-2000 BC 2000-1500 BC
		Coordinates and chronology from Meena and Tripathi (2001-2)	
Purani Marmi	Chittorgarh district (25° 06′ N, 74° 25′ E)	Ahar culture Early Historic - Medieval	1400-1500 BC
		Coordinates and chronology from Mohanty *et al.* (2000)	

Figure 3.1 Location and chronology of excavated Ahar sites in Rajasthan

Materials	Terracotta, Clay, Reused Pottery	Stone	Metal	Shell	Bone	Steatite
Some Artefact Types	Bangles Beads Miniature pots Clay sealings Dabbers Disc fragments Ear studs and spools Sling balls Figurines Game pieces Graffiti marks Hopscotches Jar stoppers Perforated discs	Bead polishers Grinding stones Hammer stones Hopscotches Querns Sling balls Weights	Bangles Bells Blades Hoe fragments Nails Points Rings	Bangles Beads Cowrie shells Inlay pieces Worked shells	Beads Ornament Point Worked bone	Beads Button Vessel fragments
Approx. Total Artefacts per Material Type	625	720*	130	180	20	175

* This number does not include the lithics (chipped stone) recovered from the site (see Raczek this volume).

Figure 3.2 Variety of artefacts discovered at Gilund during the 1999-2005 excavations

Balathal is a rural site, located about 40km northeast of Udaipur. It consists of a single mound which may have originally covered an area of 2 to 3 hectares. However, today only one-third of the original mound remains (Misra *et al.*, 1997). The rest has disappeared due to the encroaching agricultural plots of local village farmers. Balathal was excavated extensively from 1994 to 2000 by a team of archaeologists from Deccan College, Pune. There have been many articles and preliminary reports written about Balathal (e.g. Gogte 1996; Kajale 1996; Robbins *et al.*, 2007; Shinde *et al.*, 2002; Thomas and Joglekar 1996). However, specific details about the quantity and variety of material culture recovered at the site, aside from pottery, have not yet been published.

Purani Marmi is situated on the bank of the Banas River next to the modern village of Nai Marmi. The site has been badly damaged by past floods, which cut into the main mound, as well as the agricultural practices of the present villagers. A salvage excavation was conducted by a team of archaeologists from Deccan College from 1999-2000. The results of this excavation were published in an article by R.K. Mohanty *et al.* (2000). Other research at the site includes the analysis of Purani Marmi's terracotta cattle figurines by V.N. Misra *et al.* (1993).

The site of Ojiyana is somewhat unique in comparison to the other four in terms of its location. It is situated in the hilly region of the Bhilwara district of Rajasthan, well north of the other sites. Furthermore, while the majority of Ahar-Banas sites are situated close to rivers, Ojiyana is located over 14km away from the nearest river, Khari (Meena and Tripathi 2000, 68). Excavations at Ojiyana began in 1999, and detailed information and analysis of the site are still to come.

Gilund is situated one km south of the Banas River in the Rajsamand District of Rajasthan, roughly 100km northeast of Udaipur. It is comprised of two large mounds. The one in the southeast has been designated GLD-1 and that to the north as GLD-2. GLD-1 contains thick layers of Early Historic materials above Late Chalcolithic levels. GLD-2 is comprised of predominantly Chalcolithic material. The first excavations at Gilund, conducted by B. B. Lal from 1959-60, yielded antiquities such as terracotta animal figurines and gamesmen, beads of terracotta and semiprecious stone, microliths, fragments of copper and stone sling-balls, saddle-querns and rubbers (IAR 1960, 41). The 1999-2005 excavations conducted by the University of Pennsylvania and Deccan College unearthed a much larger assemblage of antiquities representing a longer range of occupation and material production at the site.

The Gilund cultural assemblage is comprised of objects of terracotta, clay, reused pottery, stone (predominantly quartzite) and semi-precious stone, metal, shell, bone and steatite (Hanlon in review). The variety of antiquities, arranged by material type, is presented in Figure 3.2. However, this list is not exhaustive. Overall, the antiquities range from Prehistoric lithics and pottery to Medieval coins.

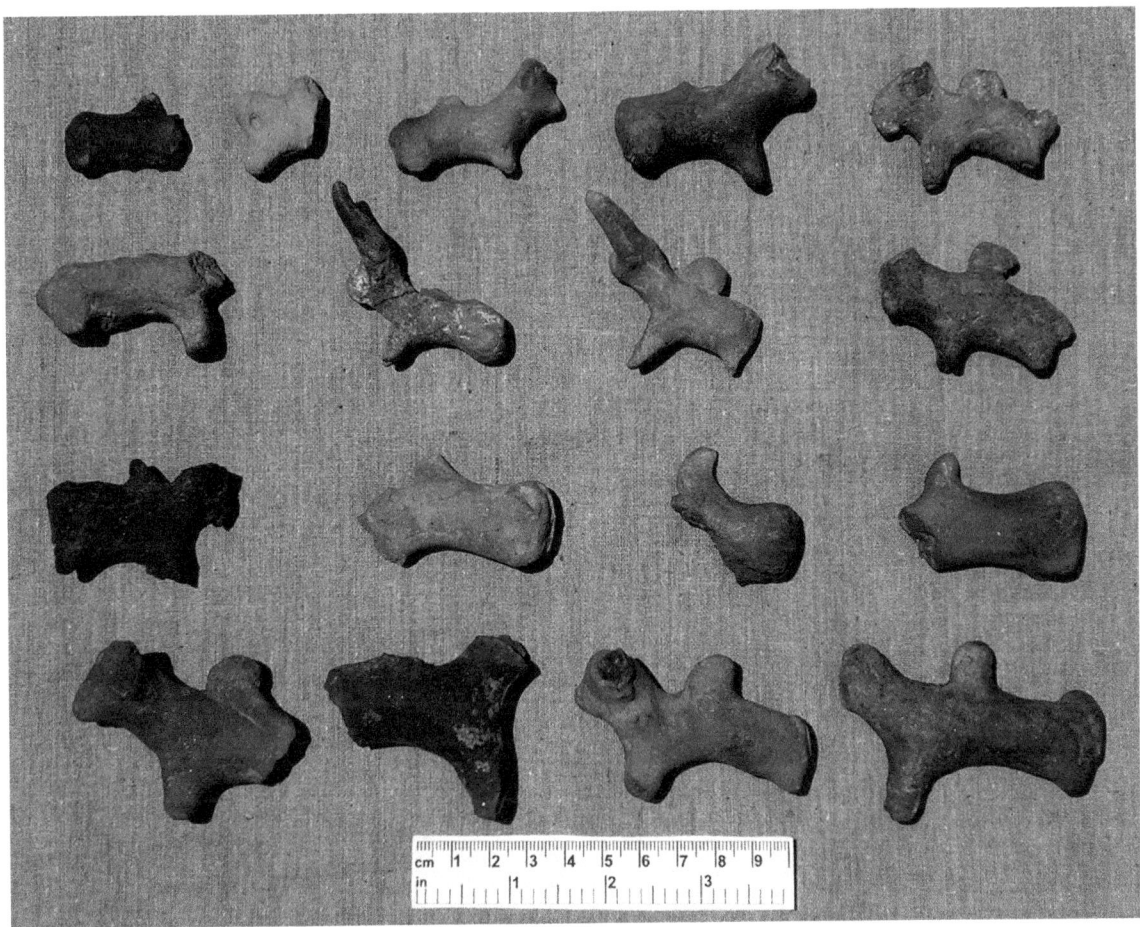

Figure 3.3 Various humped cattle figurines from Gilund (Photo taken by author)

Zoomorphic Terracotta Figurines

Excavations at Gilund yielded over 100 terracotta figurines dating from the Middle Chalcolithic to the Early Historic periods. They are most often of fired terracotta, but there are also a number of unfired clay specimens. Nearly half of the collection is comprised of humped animals, interpreted as humped cattle, or *Bos indicus*. There is significant stylistic variety within the collection, for example, the way the face, legs and hump are shaped; the range in size; whether or not the artisan added such details as ears under the horns, or incised eyes, nose and mouth, etc. (Figure 3.3). In particular, the humped cattle figurines share stylistic affinities with those recovered at Ahar (Sankalia *et al.*, 1969, Figure 109, nos. 1, 3, 4, 6, 7, 12), Ojiyana (Meena 2000; Meena and Tripathi 2002, Figures 9-11) and Purani Marmi (Misra *et al.*, 1993, Figure 1, nos. 15, 16). Similar humped cattle figurines have also been reported from Mahidpur in Madhya Pradesh (Ali *et al.*, 2004).

There are also three stylised cattle figurines from Gilund (Figure 3.4), which resemble the type found at Purani Marmi (Misra *et al.*, 1993, Figure 1, nos. 1-8) in Rajasthan, and at Kayatha (Ansari and Dhavalikar 1975, Figure 73, nos. 14, 17-22; Wakankar 1967, pl. 18) and Mahidpur (Ali *et al.*, 2004, pl. 32, nos. 10-15) in Madhya

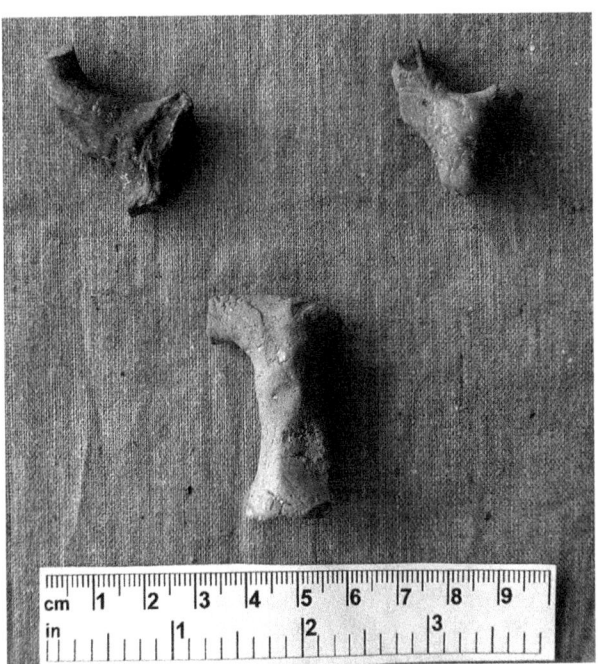

Figure 3.4 Stylised cattle figurines from Gilund (Photo taken by author)

Pradesh. In their article on the excavations at Balathal, Misra *et al.*, (1995, 70) also reported finds of terracotta

Figure 3.5 Humped cattle figurines with pointed faces from Gilund (Photo taken by author)

cattle figurines similar to those found at Purani Marmi. However, photos or drawings of these figurines from Chalcolithic levels at Balathal have not yet been published.

Like Gilund, Ojiyana is reported to have a particularly large number of terracotta cattle figurines. Parallels exist between the delicate humped cattle figurines with pointed faces found at Gilund (Figure 3.5) and those from Ojiyana (Meena 2000, 2; Meena and Tripathi 2002, Figure 9, nos. 2, 3, 5, Figure 10). What is rather interesting about the collection of figurines at Ojiyana is that over 50 of the figurines are painted white. Therefore, it may be significant that a white-painted zoomorphic figurine was also discovered at Gilund. According to B. R. Meena and Alok Tripathi, the discovery of zoomorphic figurines with modeled udders at Ojiyana may be the first depiction of cows in Chalcolithic India (Meena and Tripathi 2002, 58). A total of 12 such figurines were excavated from Ojiyana Phase II deposits. A single humped cattle figurine with modeled udders was also uncovered at Gilund from Late Chalcolithic levels (Figure 3.6).

Other Terracotta Objects

Gilund's cultural assemblage contains a large variety of other terracotta objects, many of which resemble antiquities found at Ahar. For example, there are two antiquities from Gilund that have knobbed conical tops and finger tip decoration around the edges. These were found in Middle Chalcolithic levels and have been classified as jar-stoppers. Sankalia *et al.* classified a nearly identical artefact discovered in Phase Ib at Ahar as a finial (1969, Figure 118, no. 1).

Figure 3.6 Humped cow figurine with udders from Gilund (Photo taken by author)

Another group of antiquities from Gilund, the use of which has not yet been determined, closely resemble what Sankalia *et al.* (1969) classified in the Ahar report as 'decorated pieces' and 'skin rubbers' (Sankalia *et al.*, 1969, 176-9, 188-90). However, most of the ones from Gilund are slipped, and therefore would have been

Figure 3.7 Round 'decorated pieces' from Gilund (Photo taken by author)

difficult to use as abrasives. The Gilund 'decorated pieces' appear to be broken portions of what were originally round impressed terracotta cakes, each of them averaging about 1.5cm in thickness (Figure 3.7). One possibility is that they were used to make seal impressions (Possehl *et al.*, 2004; Shinde *et al.*, 2005; and see Ameri this volume). However, no sealing bearing corresponding impressions has been discovered at Gilund, or any of the other Ahar-Banas sites (see Ameri this volume).

Other terracotta objects such as beads and spindle whorls from Gilund resemble similar objects from Ahar (Sankalia *et al.*, 1969, Figures 99-104, 111) and Ojiyana (Meena 2000, 2). In addition, 15 terracotta bangle fragments were discovered during excavations at Gilund: five from Chalcolithic levels and ten from Early Historic levels. Terracotta bangles have not yet been reported from Chalcolithic levels at any of the other excavated Ahar-Banas sites in Rajasthan.

Stone Objects

The wide variety of stone grinding tools, such as rubber stones, querns, mullers, pestles and pounders, unearthed at Gilund suggests that grain processing was a significant part of daily life. Stone tools such as polishers and hammer stones were also used in bead and lithic manufacture. Other stone antiquities from Gilund include sling balls, rounded stone discs called 'hopscotches' and large perforated stones, which may have served as weights. Similar antiquities, such as grinding stones and sling balls, have also been recovered from excavations at Ahar (Sankalia *et al.*, 1969, 207-12), Balathal (Misra *et al.*, 1997, 57) and Ojiyana (Meena and Tripathi 2001, 75-6).

Shell, Steatite and Bone Objects

The variety of shell antiquities discovered at Gilund includes shell bangles, worked shells, cowries and inlay pieces. Sixty-five of the 70 shell bangles were discovered on GLD-1, predominantly in Early Historic levels (Figure 3.8). Several are identical in design to those discovered at Ahar (Sankalia *et al.*, 1969, Figure 124, nos. 1-4). Shell bangles are also present at Ojiyana (Meena 2000, 14; Meena and Tripathi 2000, 72).

The majority of worked shells are concentrated in the Middle Chalcolithic levels on GLD-2, particularly in Trenches 34 and 35 near the bottom of the northwest slope. Seven cowrie shells were discovered during excavations on GLD-1 in Early Historic layers. A total of four shell inlay pieces, two round and two diamond-shaped, were excavated from Middle Chalcolithic and Early Historic levels.

A single conical button of white steatite paste was found in Late Chalcolithic levels at Gilund on top of GLD-2. This button appears identical to one found at Ahar in Period Ib (Sankalia *et al.*, 1969, Figure 98, no. 26). It is remarkable that despite the wide-scale use of steatite for bead making during the Chalcolithic, this is the only specimen of steatite discovered at Ahar (Sankalia *et al.*, 1969, 167). The steatite bead making industry is well represented at Gilund, with over 260 steatite beads, predominantly in the form of micro-beads. Meena and Tripathi have also reported that 'steatite beads out

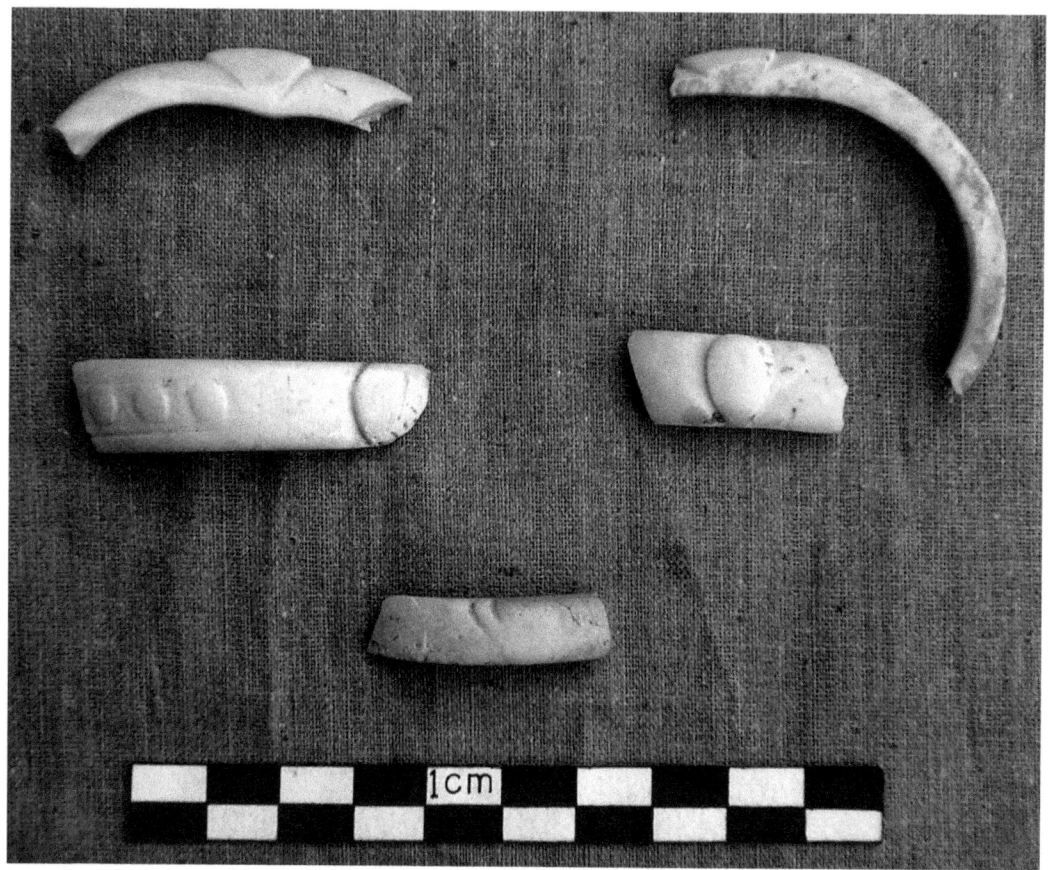

Figure 3.8 Early Historic shell bangles from Gilund (Photo taken by author)

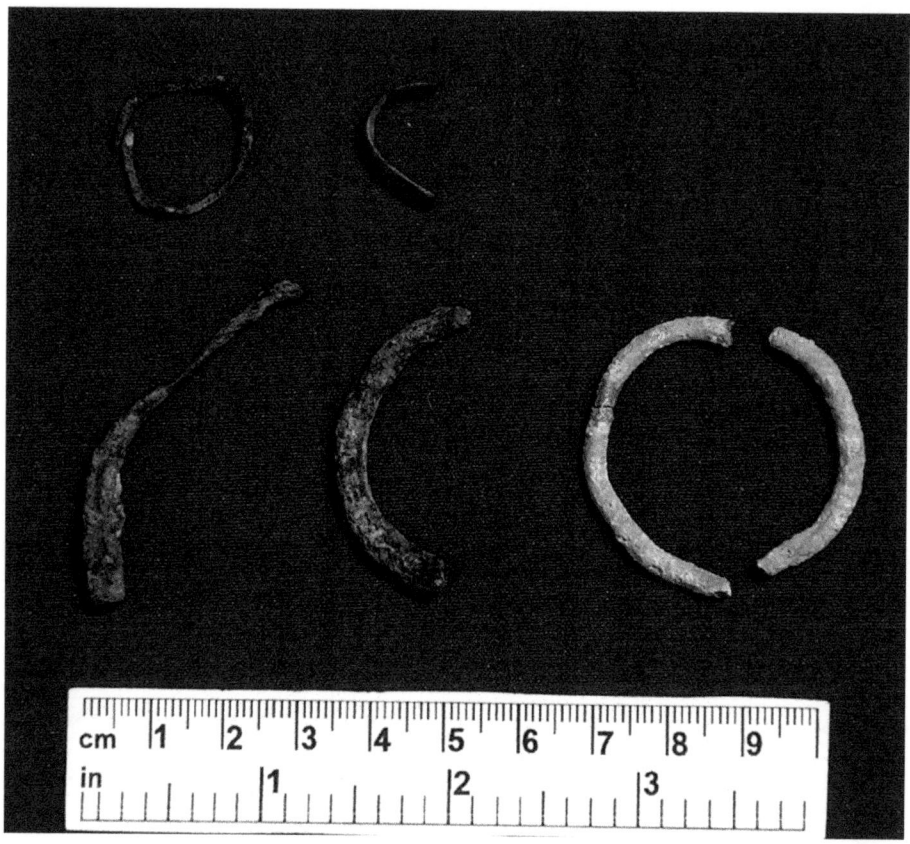

Figure 3.9 Copper objects from Gilund: 2 rings, 1 kohl stick, and 3 bangle fragments (Photo taken by author)

number beads of all other materials' at Ojiyana (Meena and Tripathi 2001, 76).

Excavations at Gilund yielded a handful of bone antiquities. Five are from Late Chalcolithic levels and include worked and polished bone, and an unidentified bone ornament. A single bone point was also discovered in Early Historic levels.

Copper Objects and Technology

The copper objects discovered at Gilund invite comparisons to the copper assemblages of Ahar, Balathal and Ojiyana (Figure 3.9). In general, copper objects from these four Ahar-Banas sites are relatively similar, particularly the kohl sticks from Gilund, Ahar (Sankalia *et al.*, 1969, Figure 121, nos. 5-6), and Balathal (Shinde 2000, Figure 6), as well as the copper rings and bangles from Gilund and Ojiyana (Meena and Tripathi 2002, pl. 16). Implements fashioned from copper sheets (Figure 3.10) are present at all the excavated Ahar-Banas sites except Purani Marmi. Mohanty *et al.* (2000) do not list any copper objects among the recovered cultural remains from the salvage excavation at Purani Marmi. However, in Rima Hooja's 1988 report, *The Ahar Culture and Beyond*, she mentions noticing some slag on the surface of the site (Hooja 1988, 210). Therefore, it is possible that such artefacts existed at Purani Marmi during the Chalcolithic but, due to the limited nature of the excavations, were not recovered.

Figure 3.10 Copper objects from Gilund: 1 knife, 1 chisel fragment, and 2 blade fragments (Photo taken by author)

Although many scholars have noted the mineral wealth of the Aravalli Range, along which many Ahar-Banas sites are located, the number of copper objects discovered is surprisingly low. At Gilund, the excavation of approximately 75 (5 x 5m) trenches over the course of five field seasons resulted in a mere total of ten copper

Figure 3.11 Copper molds from Gilund (Photo taken by author)

Figure 3.12 Vitrified crucible fragments from Gilund (Photo taken by author)

objects ascribable to the Chalcolithic: three rings, one bangle fragment, one kohl stick, two blade fragments, one chisel and two unidentified objects.

A limited range of copper antiquities were also uncovered at Ahar. Copper objects from the Chalcolithic include five rings, two bangles, three kohl sticks, four copper celts and a handful of unidentified pieces and fragments. Excavations at Ahar also revealed a circular furnace pit, approximately 1.5m in diameter and about 0.6m deep, full of white ashes and slag (Misra 1969, 300). Misra suggested that the location of the furnace in the lowermost level indicated early knowledge of metallurgy (Misra 1969, 300). This point may be significant given the discovery of a number of copper molds from Middle and Late Chalcolithic levels at Gilund (Figure 3.11). Originally, these molds were designated as lamps and containers based on the classification of similar materials from Ahar (Sankalia *et al.*, 1969, Figure 107, no. 6, Figure 115, nos. 1-3). Upon close inspection, we realised that the objects at Gilund were not lamps, but copper molds. They are similar in size and exceptionally thick to withstand the heat of the molten metal. In addition, several are broken, likely as a result of removing the copper ingot. What we originally interpreted as wick channels may have instead been used to facilitate the extraction of the ingots after cooling.

Copper technology at Gilund is also demonstrated by the presence of six vitrified fragments found in Middle to Late Chalcolithic trenches (Figure 3.12). They are blackened to the point that the clay has become like pumice, and one of the fragments still has what appear to be pieces of copper attached to the inside. It is likely that these fragments were once part of one or more crucibles used in the smelting of copper. Reconstruction was attempted, but none of the fragments fit together. Overall, this evidence indicates that despite the low number of recovered copper objects, copper technology was practiced by the inhabitants of Ahar-Banas sites in Rajasthan during the Chalcolithic.

Iron Objects

While there are a small number of copper objects from Gilund, the amount of iron objects is considerably higher. Excavations yielded around 54 iron objects and an additional 45 iron fragments. The majority were found in Early Historic contexts on GLD-1, and some in mixed levels of Chalcolithic and Early Historic materials. These antiquities, particularly the points and nails (Figure 3.13), closely resemble similar artefacts from Ahar (Sankalia *et al.*, 1969, Figure 123, nos. 1-20). According to Misra, 'a variety of iron objects like axes, adzes, chisels, spearheads, arrowheads, ploughshares, and nails have been found in large quantities' in the Early Historic at Balathal (Misra 2005, 58). Iron smelting furnaces and

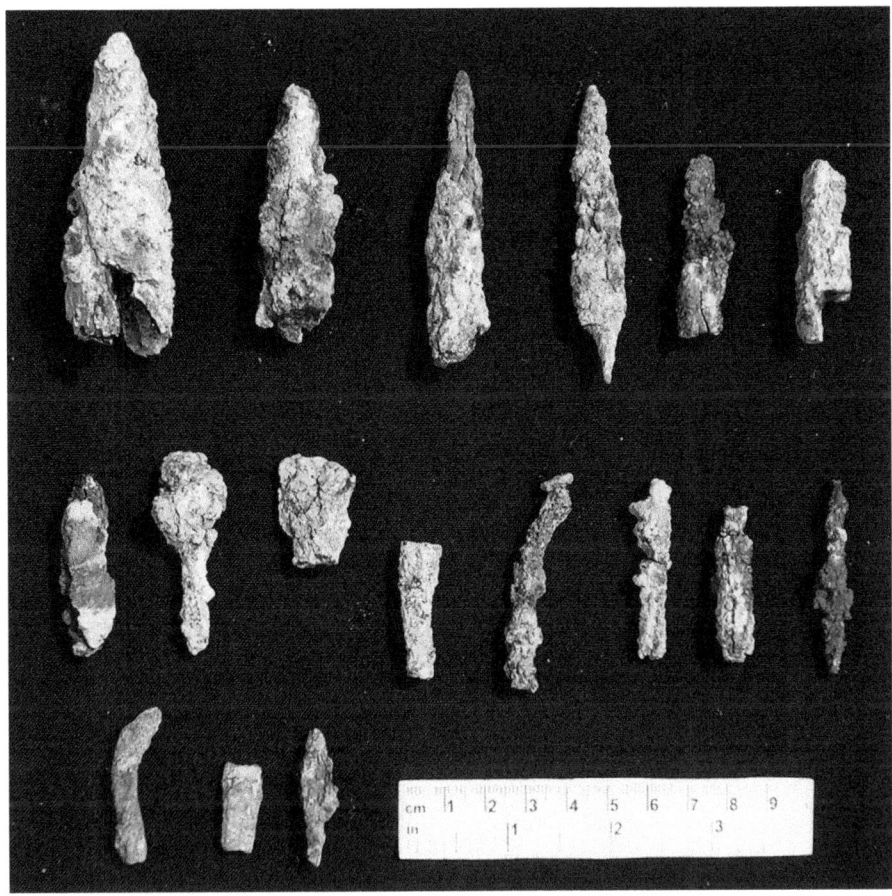

Figure 3.13 Iron points and nails from Gilund (Photo taken by author)

iron slag were also discovered at Balathal, leading excavators to suggest that it may have been an important centre for iron smelting and manufacturing during the Early Historic (Misra *et al.*, 1995, 75).

Such similarities in iron objects suggest that these sites were not only linked during the Chalcolithic period, but there may have also been considerable interaction between their inhabitants during the Early Historic period.

Summary
In conclusion, this brief overview has demonstrated that the cultural tradition of the Ahar-Banas is certainly not limited to their white-painted Black-and-Red ware. Terracotta figurines, steatite beads, stone grinding tools and evidence of copper technology have all been shown to share stylistic affinities between sites. The rich and diverse cultural assemblage of the Ahar-Banas exhibits a continuity that with further research may tell us more about social and commercial interaction in southeast Rajasthan during the third millennium BC.

Acknowledgements
I am very thankful for the guidance and advice of Dr V. S. Shinde during the classification and organisation of the Gilund antiquities, as well as the kind hospitality of the Deccan College faculty and staff. I am also grateful to Dr G. L. Possehl for his continued guidance and support.

Bibliography

Ali, R., A. Trivedi and D. Solanki. 2004. *Chalcolithic Site of Ujjain Region: Mahidpur*. Delhi, Sharada Publishing House.

Ansari, Z. D. and M. K. Dhavalikar. 1975. *Excavations at Kayatha*. Pune, Deccan College.

Archaeological Survey of India

1954-55. Ahar, District Udaipur, *Indian Archaeology: A Review* (IAR), 14-15.

1955-56. Excavation at Ahar, District Udaipur, *Indian Archaeology: A Review* (IAR), 11.

1959-60. Excavations at Gilund, District Udaipur, *Indian Archaeology: A Review* (IAR), 41-46.

1961-62. Excavations at Ahar, District Udaipur, *Indian Archaeology: A Review* (IAR), 43-44.

Gogte, V. D. 1996. Chalcolithic Balathal: A trading centre as revealed by the XRD study of pottery. *Man and Environment* 21(1), 103-10.

Hanlon, J. A. Under review. The Gilund antiquities. In V. S. Shinde, G. L. Possehl and T. Raczek (eds), *Excavations at Gilund*. Philadelphia.

Hooja, R. 1988. *The Ahar Culture and Beyond: Settlements and Frontiers of 'Mesolithic' and Early Agricultural Sites in South-eastern Rajasthan c. 3rd-2nd Millennia B.C.* British Archaeological Reports International Series 412. Oxford, British Archaeological Reports.

Kajale, M. D. 1996. Palaeobotanical investigations at Balathal: Preliminary results. *Man and Environment* 21(1), 98-102.

Meena, B. R. (ed.) 2000. *Recent Excavations in Rajasthan*. Jaipur, Archaeological Survey of India.

Meena, B. R. and A. Tripathi. 2000. Excavation at Ojiyana. *Puratattva* 30, 67-73.

Meena, B. R. and A. Tripathi. 2001. Further excavation at Ojiyana. *Puratattva* 31, 73-7.

Meena, B. R. and A. Tripathi. 2002. Excavations at Ojiyana: An unique Copper Age site in the Aravalli. *Praghdhara* 12, 45-66.

Misra, V. N. 1969. Early village communities of the Banas Basin, Rajasthan. In M. C. Pradhan, R. D. Singh, P. K. Misra and D. B. Sastry (eds), *Anthropology and Archaeology: Essays in Commemoration of Verrier Elwin, 1902-64*, 296-310. Oxford, Oxford University Press.

Misra, V. N. 2005. Radiocarbon chronology of Balathal, District Udaipur, Rajasthan. *Man and Environment* 30(1), 54-60.

Misra, V. N., V. S. Shinde, R. K. Mohanty, K. Dalal, A. Mishra, L. Pandey and J. Kharakwal. 1995. Excavations at Balathal: Their contribution to the Chalcolithic and Iron Age cultures of Mewar, Rajasthan. *Man and Environment* 20(1), 57-80.

Misra, V. N., V. S. Shinde, R. K. Mohanty and L. Pandey. 1993. Terracotta bull figurines from Marmi: A Chalcolithic settlement in Chitorgarh District, Rajasthan. *Man and Environment* 18(2), 149-52.

Misra, V. N., V. S. Shinde, R. K. Mohanty, L. Pandey and J. Kharakwal. 1997. Excavations at Balathal, Udaipur District, Rajasthan (1995-97), with special reference to Chalcolithic architecture. *Man and Environment* 22(2), 35-59.

Mohanty, R. K., A. Mishra, P. P. Joglekar, P. K. Thomas, J. Kharakwal and T. Panda. 2000. Purani Marmi: A late Ahar Culture settlement in Chitaurgarh District, Rajasthan. *Puratattva* 30, 132-41.

Possehl, G. L. and P. C. Rissman. 1992. The chronology of prehistoric India: From earliest times to the Iron Age. In R.W. Ehrich (ed.), *Chronologies in Old World Archaeology 3rd edition*, 465-90 and 447-74. Chicago, University of Chicago Press.

Possehl, G. L., V. Shinde, and M. Ameri. 2004. The Ahar-Banas Complex and the BMAC. *Man and Environment* 29(2), 18-29.

Robbins G., V. Mushrif, V. N. Misra, R. K. Mohanty and V. Shinde. 2007. Adult skeletal material from Balathal: A full report and inventory. *Man and Environment* 32(2), 1-26.

Sankalia, H. D., S. B. Deo and S. D. Ansari. 1969. *Excavations at Ahar (Tambavati)*. Pune, Deccan College.

Shinde, V. 2000. The Origin and Development of the Chalcolithic in Central India. *Indo-Pacific Prehistory Association Bulletin* 19, 125-136.

Shinde, V. and G. L. Possehl. 2005. A report on the excavations at Gilund, 1999-2001. In C. Jarrige and V. Lefèvre (eds), *South Asian Archaeology 2001*, 293-302. Paris, Éditions Recherche sur les Civilizations.

Shinde, V., G. L. Possehl and M. Ameri. 2005. Excavations at Gilund 2001-2003: The seal impressions and other finds. In U. Franke-Vogt and H. J. Weisshaar (eds), *South Asian Archaeology 2003*, 155-65. Aachen, Linden Soft Verlag.

Shinde, V., G. L. Possehl and S. Sinha-Deshpande. 2002. The ceramic assemblage in Proto-historic Mewar (Rajasthan) with special reference to Gilund and Balathal. *Puratattva* 32, 5-24.

Thomas, P. K. and P. P. Joglekar. 1996. Faunal remains from Balathal, Rajasthan: A preliminary report. *Man and Environment* 21(1), 91-97.

Wakankar, V. S. 1967. Kayatha Excavation. *Journal of Vikram University*. Special number, 1-52.

4. Cultural Developments at the Chalcolithic Site of Gilund, Rajasthan

Matthew J. Landt

Variations in subsistence strategies often demarcate cultural shifts that allow archaeologists to consider the way in which social boundaries were created and enforced (Lizee et al., 1995). This is true for foragers (Noss 1995), farmers (Weber 1996) as well as pastoralists (Humphrey and Sneath 1999). This paper is concerned with pastoralists, specifically those in the Banas River Basin of southeastern Rajasthan, and the way in which those herders may have reacted to cultural and environmental constraints within their community by shifting species composition in their herds to optimise socio-economic benefits. Recent work within the Banas River Basin, specifically at the Chalcolithic site of Gilund, provides an opportunity to focus on such community level interactions in an effort to better understand the way in which these socio-economic shifts in subsistence patterns reflect different levels of community organisation in northwest India.

Environmental data from archaeological sites in Rajasthan provide a backdrop to which shifts in animal and plant husbandry can be measured (Gifford-Gonzalez 2005; Harrison 1988). By calculating the economic impact of these shifting husbandry decisions, archaeologists can better understand the way in which communities and households perceive differential social ranking strategies. By asking and addressing questions that relate to shifting economic activities across transitional periods (i.e., pastoral to agro-pastoral economies) we will be better able to ask questions that

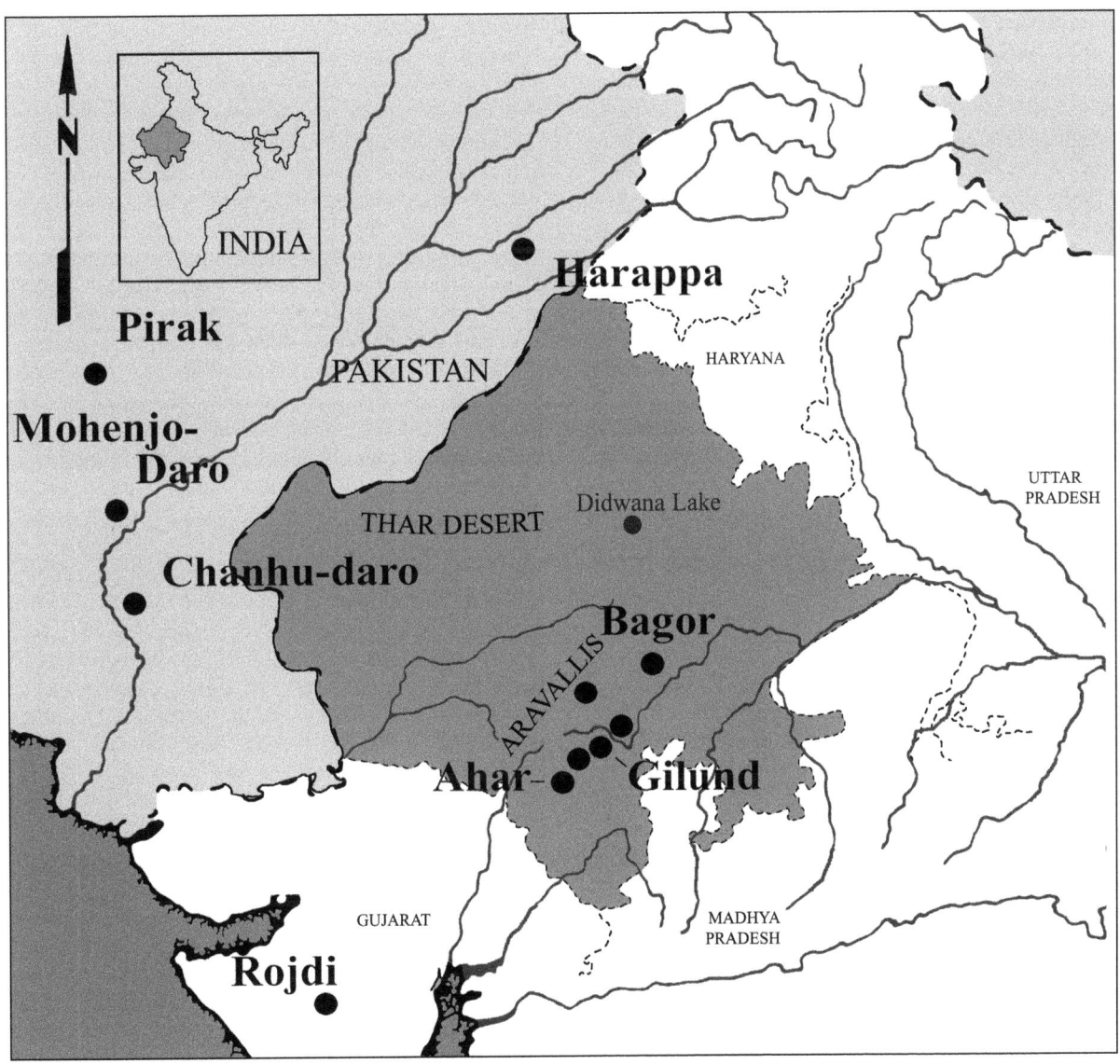

Figure 4.1. Map of Rajasthan and the surrounding areas highlighting important sites in the region

actually address the social growth and development of village communities and incorporate local people and local events into the practice of archaeological analysis (Dietler and Hayden 2001; Dornan 2002; Stein 2002, 906).

What follows is a look at the economic processes of pastoralism in the Banas River Basin utilising a cultural ecological framework in a way that highlights the development of an agro-pastoral community. I will begin by providing a general background of the Banas River drainage archaeology. This includes a general environmental chronology that serves as a foundation for discussions of economic shifts. Economic changes seen in Early Chalcolithic Banas River settlements (i.e., what to herd, where to herd, etc.) are then explained based on prehistoric environmental patterning and current ethnographic economic analogy. This paper is designed to promote discussion of shifting subsistence decisions, as embedded processes of culturally constructed notions of appropriate and reasonable behaviour (Alvard and Nolin 2002; Sosis 2002).

Regional Background

In the later part of the fourth-millennium BC, a culture with a distinctive Black-and-Red ceramic ware began occupying sites that cluster along the tributaries and main course of the Banas River (Mishra 2002-03; Sankalia *et al.*, 1969). The Banas River system lies to the south of the Thar Desert and to the west of Gujarat over the Aravalli hills (Figure 4.1). The Banas River eventually drains into the Ganges River Basin and onward into the Bay of Bengal. Roughly 100 known Chalcolithic archaeological sites are concentrated in and near the Banas River valley and are affiliated with a Banas culture (Hooja 1988; Misra 1967). However, the cultural affiliation of the peoples situated in the region of the Banas and Berach River basins is more often referred to as the Ahar Culture, after the type site at Ahar (Chakrabarti 1968; Sankalia *et al.*, 1969; IAR 1954-5, IAR 1955-6). Sites with material culture affiliations to these groups of sites are hereafter referred to as part of an Ahar-Banas Chalcolithic (ABC) Complex.

Limited excavations have occurred at only five sites in southeastern Rajasthan: Ahar (IAR 1955-6; Sankalia *et al.*, 1969), Balathal (Misra *et al.*, 1995; Misra 1997; Shinde 2000; Shinde *et al.*, 2002), Gilund (IAR 1959-60; Shinde *et al.*, 2002, 2005; Shinde and Possehl 2005), Ojiyana (Meena and Tripathi 2000, 2001-2) and Purani Marmi (Mohanty *et al.*, 1999-2000). Three sites in the Banas Basin, Ahar (Hooja 1988), Balathal (Misra 1997; Misra *et al.*, 1997, 35; Misra and Mohanty 2001, 68; Shinde *et al.*, 2002, 8), and Gilund (Possehl, personal communication) provide a radiocarbon-bounded timeframe for the Ahar-Banas Chalcolithic culture of *c.* 3000–1500 BC. Based on ceramic analysis, this 1500-year time period is then subdivided into three phases: Early (*c.* 3000–2500 BC), Mature (*c.* 2500–2000 BC) and Late (*c.* 2000–1700 BC) (Possehl and Rissman 1992). All of these excavations have shown that the people affiliated with the Ahar-Banas Culture lived in small settlements with an agro-pastoral economy that was supplemented with hunting and gathering. Archaeological evidence suggests that they built structures on stabilised sand dunes during the early occupations. Later construction included finer-shaped stonework and mud-bricks that was then replaced with coarser construction towards the end of the period. Professor Shinde and others (2002) believe that these settlements were socially organised around a central authority with evidence of social stratification and economic hierarchies.

Three sites in the Banas River Basin are detailed below, as they are central to the discussions herein. Two of the sites are excavated ABC Complex sites (Ahar and Gilund), and the third, Bagor, is the most well known habitation in the Banas River Basin that spans the pre-Chalcolithic/Chalcolithic transition (Misra 1973, 1997).

Bagor

Bagor is a microlithic site in southeastern Rajasthan that was initially occupied at approximately 5500 BC and therefore pre-dates the Chalcolithic occupation of the Banas River Basin (Misra 1973, 1997; Possehl *et al.*, 2004; Thomas 1977; Thomas and Joglekar 1994). Economically, those who inhabited Bagor were supported by pastoral activities, as indicated by Dr Thomas' (1977) faunal analysis. Dr Thomas and others (Allchin and Allchin 1982, Clason 1981) have noted a reliance upon sheep and goat (64%) with lesser usage of larger stock (17% cattle and buffalo) and mixed wild game (12% Nilgai, antelope/gazelle, rabbit, mongoose, fox and fish) in the pre-Chalcolithic portions of the site. While there are some questions regarding the economic agendas of the different groups who occupied the site, excavations at Bagor have helped establish the small-stock economic focus of individuals who lived in the Banas River Basin (as throughout Rajasthan) before the ABC Complex.

Ahar

Ahar is the type-site of third-millennium occupation in the Banas River Basin. It is located in the city of Udaipur, and is locally known as Dhulkot (Hooja 1988, 44). Before modern construction in Udaipur, the site overlooked the Ahar River (Hooja 1988, 44). Trial excavations were initiated on the 12.8m tall mound in 1952 and resumed in 1953 (IAR 1954-5, 1955-6). The site was then re-excavated in 1961-2 by the late Prof. H. D. Sankalia (1969). Recovered faunal remains indicate the utilisation of wild and domestic animals, with cattle marking the bulk of the remains (78%), though a smaller number of buffalo (1%), sheep/goat (8%), pig (wild and domestic, 4%) and dog (4%) also occur throughout the occupation (Shah 1969). Identified wild animals include deer (4%), mongoose (<1%), fowl (<1%), fish (<1%) and turtle (<1%) (Shah 1969). Thus, the available evidence indicates that throughout the occupation of Ahar, the community focused its attention towards the utilisation of domestic large-stock animals.

Gilund

The site of Gilund covers approximately 25 hectares and is considered to be one of the larger ABC Complex sites. Shinde and Possehl (2005) have referred to Gilund as an important economic and political centre for the ABC Complex and have suggested that Gilund was situated with the intent of maximising the products of an agro-pastoral lifeway (see also Shinde this volume). While much of the excavated material from Gilund remains to be formally analysed, qualitative datasets can be used in an effort to better understand the formation processes of the agro-pastoral economy at Gilund. Since quantitative records of species composition across the site have not been undertaken, information regarding specific NISPs (Numbers of Identified Specimens) and MNIs (Minimum Numbers of Individuals) are not available. Qualitatively, however, recovered faunal remains indicate a preference for domestic animals over their wild counterparts, with large-stock (cattle and buffalo) clearly dominating the assembly. Numerous remains of sheep/goat are also present, as are a scattering of wild animals (blackbuck and other wild cervids, rabbits, rodents, snakes, birds, fishes, bivalves and snails).

Pastoralism as Risk Management

Economically, shifts in pastoral economies are often seen as fiscal management strategies designed to reduce overall risk and increase the amount of caloric return on one's labour investment (Alvard and Kuznar 2001; Mishra 2005; Russell 1988). Risk-reduction strategies are currently used to explain why modern census numbers of sheep and goat from Rajasthan—increasing at a rate of 17.6% and 12.4% respectively during the drying trend of the 1990s—indicate that the herding of sheep provides greater modern compensation even though goats reproduce faster (Alvard and Kuznar 2001; UNDP 2002). In an economically narrow way, when herders differentially maintain the species composition of their herds, species should be maintained in order of their respective return rates, which includes the acquisition and processing of milk (Russell 1988). These return rates should be ranked according to social and economic values, though they are often understood and measured by archaeologists in kcals, which are frequently perceived as the short-term payoffs. Kenneth Russell (1988) took a long-term perspective on animal husbandry in his dissertation and arrived at species-ranked kcal numbers by including more than just meat weights and values. Russell included the amount of daily time allocated to different tasks as well as differential labour input from family members. These tasks included the gathering of secondary animal by-products such as milk and fur by an individual family member for an individual herd animal throughout the animals' domestic life expectancy. As such, and regardless of other social parameters, kcal returns are higher for larger animals, where cattle, sheep and goat respectively return 897, 374, and 252 kcal per hour of labour input (Russell 1988, 105-6). If this were the only basis for pastoral decisions, large animals should be maintained in equally sized herds over small animals.

These return rates are, however, offset by the autonomous nature of growth among biological organisms where a pastoralist starting with two animals could increase that herd to 100 animals in 24 years for goats, 40 years for sheep, and 72 years for cattle (Alvard and Kuznar 2001, Table 3). By correcting kcal return rates with reproductive rates, the faster reproduction of small-stock (goats and sheep) compensates for their increased labour requirements and lower individual return rates per animal (Alvard and Kuznar 2001). This is especially true in an unstable environment where the greater reproductive rate of small-stock can quickly offset losses accrued during droughts and predation events. Alvard and Kuznar (2001) have also hypothesised that it is the greater reproduction rate of small-stock that provides ample reason for their early domestication.

Ethnographic evidence also indicates that the social behaviour of small-stock animals allows them to be more easily maintained in greater numbers by a single herder than are large-stock animals. This is especially true for sheep, where their gregarious nature more than compensates a pastoralist for what is otherwise a middling birth rate and kcal return rate (Figure 4.2). Modern analogy among pastoral groups in Tibet (Namgail *et al.*, 2007), the Middle East (Khazanov 1980), East Africa (Gebre-Mariam 1988), Algeria (Trautmann 1985) and Mongolia (Humphrey and Sneath 1999; Khazanov 1980) indicate that a single herder can readily maintain a flock of approximately 300 sheep, 150 goats or a herd of 50 cattle with the same approximate energy output. Thus, environmental and cultural parameters not withstanding, small-stock are the single best economically viable alternative for pastoralists.

Economic Variables	kcal/hr[1]	births/year[2]	manageable herd size/shepherd[3]	ca. kcal/herd
Cattle	897	0.5	50-100	67,300
Sheep	374	1.5	300-400	131,000
Goat	252	2.0	100-200	37,800

[1] Russell 1988
[2] Alvard and Kuznar 2001; UNDP 2002
[3] Gebre-Mariam 1988; Khazanov 1980; Trautmann 1985

Figure 4.2. Economic variables for cattle, sheep, and goats ranked by kcal/hr

Environmental Parameters

Environmental parameters such as the amount of available nutrition and standing biomass dictate the maximum animal population size, or sustainable animal yield, that the landscape can support (Alvard and Kuznar 2001; Binford 2001; Clark 1984, 1985; Trautmann 1985; Wienpahl 1985). In other words, when vegetation is plentiful, wild animals abound and pastoral herds can be allowed to grow. Conversely, when available vegetation decreases and fodder becomes scarce, herders are better off focusing maintenance activities on a selected set of their own resources. Thus, standing biomass is likely to be a large controlling factor for available prey species, whether herded or hunted.

The relative nutritional value and standing biomass of a prehistoric landscape is difficult to operationalise in meaningful ways. However, shifting climatic regimes are a useful proxy for such environmental parameters and can provide a means of better understanding the conditions under which individuals and communities operated. Recent climatological work off of the coast of Oman and at Didwana (a lake at the northeast end of the Aravalli range) provide a coarse measure of summer monsoon strength across the Indian Ocean and serves as proxy measures for the amount of aridity in the Banas River Basin (Gupta *et al.*, 2003; Kajale *et al.*, 2004).

Gupta *et al.*, (2003) present a continuous record of shifts in *G. bulloides* from sediment cores in the seabed off the coast of Oman that identifies strong and weak interregional weather patterns. The bulk of their research links southwest Asian monsoon variability with temperature shifts in the North Atlantic region and provides a persistent centennial scale measurement of global climate change. While their record is difficult to fine-tune for cultural time periods in the last 5000 years, it provides general trends that are useful in demonstrating periods of variability in the southwest Asian monsoons.

A more detailed and local record is provided by Kajale *et al.*'s (2004) geomorphological, palynological and stable isotopic analysis of sediments from numerous playas across the Thar Desert. They note that the Thar Desert was a difficult place for humans to live during the Pleistocene, though pluvial shifts during the Holocene allowed for a more stable, if not nomadic, human presence. With moderate summer and winter monsoons, adequate water and developed stream channels, the Thar landscape supported an increased level of usable biomass between the sixth and fourth-millenniums BC. This increase in moisture notably dropped during the second-millennium BC when summer and winter monsoons weakened (Kajale *et al.*, 2004, 93).

Economic Shifts in the Banas River Basin

During the end of the fourth-millennium BC (approximately 3300-3000 BC) the summer monsoons increased in strength (Gupta *et al.*, 2003). The increase in moisture that likely followed lasted until roughly 2500 BC and is documented elsewhere across India (Ajithprasad 2004; Gupta *et al.*, 2003). This heightened moisture regime coincides with an economic shift in Early Chalcolithic communities in the Banas River Basin (Thomas and Joglekar 1996). During the increased moisture regime and concomitant rise in available standing biomass, pastoralists would have been presented a series of economic choices during the fourth-millennium BC. Pastoral families would be presented the option of 'trading-up' from time intensive small-stock to what may have been viewed as labour and space saving large-stock. Assuming pastoralists wished only to increase their kcal profit margin and that household decision-making could be simplified into a few choices regarding herd management, pastoralists should either a) increase their numbers of small-stock or b) shift to a larger stock focus. Given the results in Figure 4.2, it would seem most appropriate for a pastoral family to increase their number of small-stock as it can occur quickly and therefore produce a higher return rate. As Wood (1985, 25) has noted for other pastoral groups, without a readily available market, 'Livestock production for consumption is a matter of numbers'.

A shift in herd composition, beyond that manageable by a single herder, necessitates an increase in human labour and an increase in pasture land/fodder. Many pastoral and agricultural families enlist extra aid to manage herds by recruiting children and extended family members into their work force (Gebre-Mariam 1988). Enlisting and/or coordinating with neighbors are also useful strategies, although extra-familial associations are most widely used when grazing lands are limited (Namgail *et al.*, 2007). The increase in pasture land/fodder is potentially more difficult to operationalise as it relies on the availability of green resources, be they contained in communal pasture areas, individually owned fields or market economies (Humphrey and Sneath 1999).

As previously noted, archaeofaunal evidence from the site of Bagor indicates that the economy in the Banas River drainage was designed around small-stock pastoralism (*c.* 64%) with some usage of large-stock (*c.* 17%) and wild game (*c.* 12%). During the increased moisture regime that correlates with the Early Chalcolithic, archaeozoological evidence from Ahar indicates a shift in economic focus. Chalcolithic sites in the Banas River Basin begin relying heavily on domesticated large-stock animals (*c.* 86%) with lesser usage of small-stock (*c.* 9%) and a decreasing percentage of wild animals (*c.* 4%).

Given a stable or flourishing environment, where the greater fecundity of small-stock may be negligible, economically minded pastoralists of the Early Chalcolithic shift their focus to labour saving large-stock and their larger consummate kcal return rates. This decision may be further reinforced with an increasing human population in the Banas River Basin that is indicated by an increasing number of sites during the Chalcolithic near Gilund (Dasgupta 2005, and see this volume) and the decreasing use of wild game. An increasing human population might be one of the few parameters that acts to prohibit the large herd sizes necessary to make small-stock pastoralism economically practical (Namgail 2007). As such, the shift from small to large-stock suggests that herd size and herd composition is limited more by cultural constraints, such as family size (number of employees) and population pressures (size of interactive community and limits on grazing lands), than by natural environmental parameters (herd fodder) during the Pastoral-Agro-Pastoral transition.

During the Mature Chalcolithic the summer monsoons weakened while Didwana continued to maintain perennial lake filling until roughly 2000 BC (Kajale et al., 2004). In this relatively unstable environment, pastoralists would have recovered from drought and predation losses faster by utilising the higher fecundity of smaller stock. Chalcolithic families did not shift to small-stock, but rather maintained their focus on large-stock animals. An increasing number of Chalcolithic sites, and presumably people, around Gilund would have acted to prohibit the large herd size necessary to make a shift to small-stock worthwhile (Dasgupta 2005; Namgail et al., 2007). To increase the economic output of a pastoral economy in the face of a 'full' pastoral countryside, families wishing to increase the kcal return rates of their herds would have needed to strive to increase the available biomass of the landscape.

After their reliance on large-stock animals, during the relatively brief hiatus in summer monsoon strength of the Mature Chalcolithic in the 3rd millennium BC, Chalcolithic peoples began relying more heavily on domesticated plants such as millets and wheats that were introduced into the economy of Banas River Basin communities (Kajale 1996, 101; Misra et al., 1997, 58; Sankalia et al., 1969, 229-35). Planting crops acts to further circumscribe the pastoral landscape, perpetuating the economic viability of large-stock herds. Thus, the transition from the Early to the Mature Chalcolithic marks a strong local shift from what was mainly a large-stock pastoral economy to an agro-pastoral lifeway in the Banas River Basin (Kajale 1996; Meena and Tripathi 2001; Shinde and Possehl 2005).

By focusing on smaller herds of larger stock, which take up less space, and by increasing the fodder capacity of the land (double cropping of plant domesticates) pastoral families were able to reify and maintain community growth. The maintenance of large-stock focused herds was likely to be further reinforced in light of the secondary labour advantages that are acquired from draught animals (Miller 2003, 2006). Thus, during the Mature Chalcolithic, environmental shifts were likely to be of less concern to the economic welfare of Banas River Basin communities than were cultural boundaries.

Summer monsoons continued to weaken at the end of the Mature Chalcolithic at the same time that winter monsoon precipitation fell (Gupta et al., 2003). This coincides, during the Late Chalcolithic, with increased salinity and desiccation of the nearby lake Didwana and the establishment of the monsoonal precipitation pattern that is seen today in northwest India (Kajale et al., 2004). While the archaeofaunal evidence indicates little change in herd stock composition, rice is incorporated into the subsistence strategy of the Chalcolithic peoples at roughly 2100 BC (Vishnu-Mittre 1969, 1974). The inclusion of a water-dependent plant during a drying trend can be taken as further evidence of the priority of cultural concerns over environmental parameters. The inclusion of rice may also indicate the use of irrigation and be an indicator of why sites like Gilund came to be established as hubs in an expanding economic network.

Discussion

The Early Chalcolithic marks a time of economic transition (from pastoralism to agro-pastoralism) for those who dwell in the Banas River Basin. By the Mature Chalcolithic (3rd and 2nd millennium BC) domesticated animal utilisation characterises agricultural sites such that domestic stock, as with the Harappan faunal material, accounts for greater than 80% of the Chalcolithic faunal assemblages (Meadow and Patel 2002, 2003; Thomas 1977, 2002). During the same time period, the environmental data from Rajasthan indicates trends in available biomass that should have impacted the economic decisions of local pastoral people. Yet the faunal remains from the Banas River Basin indicate economic shifts in husbandry practices that were counter-intuitive, and non-optimal in terms of kcal expenditures, when viewed in light of the environmental trends. Thus, it is clear that economic decisions during the 3rd and 2nd millennium BC were being impacted more heavily by socio-cultural than environmental parameters.

While this paper has mostly looked at pastoralism as a rational behaviour in a cultural ecological sense, it is clear that subsistence decisions (i.e., where to herd, what to herd, when to harvest, etc.) can be, and often are, embedded in culturally constructed notions of appropriate behaviour (Alvard and Nolin 2002; Sosis 2002; Sosis and Ruffle 2004). The shifting environmental and economic parameters are important in understanding the communities of the Banas River Basin, yet it is also important to note the way in which this research begins to address differing levels of community interactions.

As such, culturally embedded and constructed information can alter and/or reorient decision-making processes that might otherwise be rational economic behaviours (Dornan 2002; Hodder and Cessford 2004; Sosis 2002; Wood 1985, 24). The 3rd millennium in the Banas River Basin marks a time of economic and social transition. Social boundaries were certainly present and purposively maintained within the economies of the Banas River Basin. Yet there is more potential for conflict from social tension and subsistence risk during the Chalcolithic after the pastoral to agro-pastoral transition (Hegmon 1994). By increasing social networks of sharing and exchange, either at a familial or community level, individuals can mitigate the increasing pressures of scalar stress (Johnson 1982). As such, visible identifiers of social networks are more important in larger communities, such as Gilund, as individuals seek to distinguish themselves, alleviate social tensions, and minimise the socially sanctioned redistribution of their resources (Fox 1987; Hegmon 1994, 172). With an increasing number of face-to-face interactions during the Chalcolithic, we might expect an increase in social boundaries that were expressed symbolically in other mediums (i.e., architecture and ceramic designs). Discussion of those data sets is beyond the means of this paper, yet the potential identification of group solidarity and definable social boundaries from symbolically expressive materials holds much promise in furthering our understanding of local cultural development.

Conclusions

It is critical to understand why human populations shift between modes of subsistence strategies as we live in a growing global economy with consistently smaller 'commons' and an increased stress on cooperative activities (Agrawal 1994; Alvard and Nolin 2002; Sosis and Ruffle 2004; Wood 1985). With pastoralism declining worldwide, studying a growing Rajasthani population (both human [1.5% annually] and livestock [13% annually]) may provide a unique opportunity to ethnographically understand social interactions that reinforce agro-pastoralism as a successful mode of subsistence within reduced grazing lands in a climate that is tending towards aridity (Köller-Rollefson 1994, 4; UNDP 2002, World Bank 2006).

This paper suggests that the socio-cultural developments at Gilund can be understood by identifying economic trade-offs in herd compositions through time and identifying what local pastoralists considered to be optimum resources in their herds. The identification of shifting herd management practices then allows for the identification of cultural constraints and social boundaries within pastoral communities. As such, better understandings of variations between environmental and social contexts allow archaeologists to consider the way in which the internal social boundaries of a community were created and enforced. Simply put, cultural interactions during the Chalcolithic of southeast Rajasthan can be better understood by utilising economic models grounded in cultural ecological understandings of how and why culture groups modify social boundaries and thus incorporate people and local events into the practice of archaeological analyses.

Bibliography

Agrawal, A. 1994. I don't need it, but you can't have it: Politics on the commons. In I. Köller-Rollefson (ed.), *A Collection of Papers from Gujarat and Rajasthan*, 36-55. London, Pastoral Development Network, Overseas Development Institute.

Ajithprasad, P. 2004. Holocene adaptations of the Mesolithic and Chalcolithic settlements in North Gujarat. In Y. Yasuda and V. Shinde (eds), *Monsoon and Civilization*, 115-32. New Delhi, Roli Books Pvt. Ltd..

Allchin, B. and F. R. Allchin. 1982. *The Rise of Civilization in India and Pakistan*. New York, Cambridge University Press.

Alvard, M. S. and L. Kuznar. 2001. Deferred harvests: The transition from hunting to animal husbandry. *American Anthropologist* 103(2), 295-311.

Alvard, M. S. and D. A. Nolin. 2002. Rousseau's whale hunt? Coordination among big-game hunters. *Current Anthropology* 4(4), 533-59.

Archaeological Survey of India
1954-55. Ahar, District Udaipur. *Indian Archaeology: A Review* (IAR), 14-15.
1955-56. Excavation at Ahar, District Udaipur. *Indian Archaeology: A Review* (IAR), 11.
1957-58. Exploration in Districts Bhilwara, Chitorgarh and Udaipur. *Indian Archaeology: A Review* (IAR), 43-5.
1959-60. Excavations at Gilund, District Udaipur. *Indian Archaeology: A Review* (IAR), 41-6.

Binford, L. R. 2001. *Constructing Frames of Reference: An Analytical Method for Archaeological Theory Building Using Hunter-Gatherer and Environmental Data Sets*. Berkeley, University of California Press.

Chakrabarti, D. K. 1968. Origin of Ahar culture. *Man in India* 48(2), 97-105.

Clark, N. T. 1984. Some probable effects of drought on flock structure and production parameters in North Western Afghanistan. *Nomadic Peoples* 15, 67-74.

1985. The effect of the 1973/74 drought in Somalia on subsequent exports and registered slaughterings of camels, sheep, goats and cattle. *Nomadic Peoples* 17, 53-7.

Clason, A. T. 1981. Animal-man relationship in southern Asia during the Holocene. In B. Allchin (ed.), *South Asian Archaeology 1981: Proceedings of the Sixth International Conference of the Association of South Asian Archaeologists*, 341-3. London, Cambridge University Press.

Dasgupta, D. 2005. Site catchment analysis of the Chalcolithic settlement of Gilund in the Banas Basin. *Puratattva* 35, 102-10.

Dietler, M. and B. Hayden 2001. Digesting the feast: Good to eat, good to drink, good to think. In M. Dietler and B. Hayden (eds), *Feasts: Archaeological and Ethnographic Perspectives on Food, Politics, and Power*, 1-20. 3rd ed. Smithsonian Series in Archaeological Inquiry, B. Smith and R. Adams, general eds. Washington D.C., Smithsonian Institution Press.

Dornan, J. L. 2002. Agency and archaeology: Past, present, and future directions. *Journal of Archaeological Method and Theory* 9(4), 303-29.

Fox, J. M. 1987. Livestock ownership patterns in a Nepali village. *Mountain Research and Development* 7(2), 169-72.

Gebre-Mariam, A. 1988. Labour inputs and time allocation among the Afar. *Nomadic Peoples* 23, 37-56.

Gifford-Gonzalez, D. 2005. Pastoralism and its consequences. In A. B. Stahl (ed.), *African*

Archaeology: A Critical Introduction, 187-224. Malden, Blackwell Publishing.

Gupta, A. K., D. M. Anderson and J. T. Overpeck 2003. Abrupt changes in the Asian southwest monsoon during the Holocene and their links to the North Atlantic ocean. *Nature* 421(23), 354-7.

Harrison, G. A. 1988. Seasonality and human population biology. In I. de Garine and G. Harrison (eds), *Coping With Uncertainty in Food Supply*, 26-31. New York, Oxford University Press.

Hegmon, M. 1994. Boundary-making strategies in early Pueblo societies: style and architecture in the Kayenta and Mesa Verde regions. In W. H. Wills and R. D. Leonard (eds), *The Ancient Southwestern Community: Models and Methods for the Study of Prehistoric Social Organization*, 171-90. Albuquerque, University of New Mexico Press.

Hodder, I. and C. Cessford 2004. Daily practice and social memory at Çatalhöyük. *American Antiquity* 69(1), 17-40.

Hooja, R. 1988. *The Ahar Culture and Beyond: Settlements and Frontiers of 'Mesolithic' and Early Agricultural Sites in South-Eastern Rajasthan c. 3rd - 2nd Millennia B.C.* British Archaeological Reports International Series 412. Oxford, British Archaeological Reports.

Humphrey, C. and D. Sneath 1999. *The End of Nomadism? Society, State and the Environment in Inner Asia*. Central Asia Book Series. Durham, Duke University Press.

Johnson, G. A. 1982. Organizational structure and scalar stress. In C. Renfrew, M. J. Rowlands and B. A. Segraves (eds), *Theory and Explanation in Archaeology*, 389-421. New York, Academic Press.

Kajale, M. D. 1996. Paleobotanical investigations at Balathal: Preliminary results. *Man and Environment* 21(1), 98-102.

Kajale, M. D., B. C. Deotare and S. N. Rajaguru. 2004. Palaeomonsoons and palaeoclimatic background to the prehistoric cultures of the western and central Thar Desert, Rajasthan, Northwestern India. In Y. Yasuda and V. Shinde (eds), *Monsoon and Civilization*, 83-98. New Delhi, Roli Books Pvt. Ltd..

Khazanov, A. M. 1980. The size of herds among pastoral nomads. *Nomadic Peoples* 7, 8-13.

Köller-Rollefson, I. 1994. *Rajasthan and Gujarat: A Collection of Papers from Gujarat and Rajasthan*. London, Pastoral Development Network, Overseas Development Institute.

Lizee, J. M., H. Neff and M. D. Glascock 1995. Clay acquisition and vessel distribution patterns: Neutron activation analysis of late Windsor and Shantok tradition ceramics from southern New England. *American Antiquity* 60(3), 515-30.

Meadow, R. H. and A. K. Patel 2002. From Mehrgarh to Harappa and Dholivira: Prehistoric pastoralism in northwestern South Asia through the Harappan Period. In S. Settar and R. Korisettar (eds), *Protohistory - Archaeology of the Harappan Civilization*, 391-408. Indian Archaeology in Retrospect, Vol. II. New Delhi, Indian Council of Historical Research and Manohar.

Meadow, R. H. and A. K. Patel 2003. Prehistoric pastoralism in northwestern South Asia from the Neolithic through the Harappan Period. In S. A. Weber and W. R. Belcher (eds), *Indus Ethnobiology: New Perspectives from the Field*, 65-93. Lanham, Lexington Press.

Meena, B. R. and A. Tripathi 2000. Excavation at Ojiyana. *Puratattva* 30, 67-73.

2001-2. Excavations at Ojiyana: An unique Copper Age site in Aravalli. *Journal of the U. P. State Archaeological Department* 12, 45-66.

Miller, L. J. 2003. Secondary products and urbanism in South Asia: The evidence for traction at Harappa. In S. A. Weber and W. R. Belcher (eds), *Indus Ethnobiology: New Perspectives from the Field*, 251-325. Lanham, Lexington Press.

Miller, L. J. 2006. Secondary products and urban provisioning: Regional economies and the Indus Civilisation. Poster presented at ICAZ 2006, Mexico City, August 23-28, 2006.

Mishra, A. 2002-3. The first farming community of South-Eastern Rajasthan. *Pragdhara: Journal of the U.P. State Archaeology Department* 13, 1-27.

Mishra, C. 2005. *Pastoralism and Wildlife Conservation in the Trans-Himalaya*. Nature Conservation Foundation - Research and Conservation. Available online at http://www.ncf-india.org/projects/highalt/pastoralism.htm. Accessed May 5, 2005.

Misra, V. N. 1967. *Pre- and Protohistory of the Berach Basin, South Rajasthan*. Deccan College Postgraduate and Research Institute, Pune.

Misra, V. N. 1973. Bagor: a late Mesolithic settlement in North-West India. *World Archaeology* 5(1), 92-110.

Misra, V. N. 1997. Balathal: a Chalcolithic settlement in Mewar, Rajasthan, India: Results of first three season's excavation. *South Asian Studies* 13, 251-73.

Misra, V. N., V. Shinde, R. K. Mohanty, K. Dalal, A. Mishra, L. Pandey and J. Kharakwal 1995. Excavations at Balathal: their contribution to the Chalcolithic and Iron Age cultures of Mewar, Rajasthan. *Man and Environment* 20(1), 57-80.

Misra, V. N., V. Shinde, R. K. Mohanty, L. Pandey, and J. Kharakwal 1997. Excavations at Balathal, Udaipur District, Rajasthan (1995-1997), with special reference to Chalcolithic architecture. *Man and Environment* 22(2), 35-59.

Misra, V. N. and R. K. Mohanty 2001. A rare Chalcolithic pottery cache from Balathal, Rajasthan. *Man and Environment* 26(2), 67-74.

Mohanty, R. K., A. Mishra, P. P. Joglekar, P. K. Thomas, J. Kharakwal and T. Panda 1999-2000. Purani Marmi: A late Ahar culture settlement in Chitaurgarh District, Rajasthan. *Puratattva* 30, 132-141.

Namgail, T., Y. V. Bhatnagar, C. Mishra and S. Bagchi 2007. Pastoral nomads of the Indian Changthang: Production system, land use and socioeconomic change. *Human Ecology* 35, 497-504.

Noss, A. J. 1995. *Duikers, Cables, and Nets: A Cultural Ecology of Hunting in a Central African Forest*. Unpublished Ph.D. Dissertation, University of Florida.

Possehl, G. L., V. Shinde and M. Ameri 2004. The Ahar-Banas complex and the BMAC. *Man and Environment* 29(2), 18-29.

Possehl, G. L. and P. C. Rissman 1992. The chronology of prehistoric India: From earliest times to the Iron Age. In R. W. Ehrich (ed.), *Chronologies in Old World Archaeology*, 465-490. Vol. 1. Chicago, University of Chicago Press.

Russell, K. W. 1988. *After Eden: The Behavioral Ecology of Early Food Production in the Near East and North Africa*. British Archaeological Reports International Series 391. Oxford, British Archaeological Reports.

Sankalia, H. D., S. B. Deo and Z. D. Ansari 1969. *Excavations at Ahar 1961-1962*. Pune, Deccan College Postgraduate and Research Institute.

Shah, D. R. 1969. Animal remains from excavations at Ahar. In H. D. Sankalia, S. B. Deo and Z. D. Ansari (eds), *Excavations at Ahar 1961-1962*, 237-45. Pune, Deccan College.

Shinde, V. 2000. The origin and development of the Chalcolithic in Central India. *Indo-Pacific Prehistory Association Bulletin* 19, 125-36.

Shinde, V., G. L. Possehl and S. S. Deshpande 2002. The ceramic assemblage in Proto-Historic Mewar (Rajasthan) with special reference to Gilund and Balathal. *Puratattva* 32, 5-24.

Shinde, V. and G. L. Possehl 2005. A report on the excavations at Gilund, 1999-2001. In C. Jarrige and V. Lefèvre (eds), *South Asian Archaeology 2001: Proceedings of the Sixteenth International Conference of the European Association of South Asian Archaeologists*, 293-309. Vol. 1 Prehistory. Paris, Éditions Recherche sur les Civilisations.

Shinde, V., G. L. Possehl and M. Ameri 2005. Excavations at Gilund 2001-2003: The seal impressions and other finds. In U. Franke-Vogt and H.-J. Weisshaar (eds), *South Asian Archaeology 2003: Proceedings of the Seventeenth International Conference of the European Association of South Asian Archaeologists*, 159-69. Bonn, Linden Soft Verlag.

Sosis, R. 2002. Patch choice decisions among Ifaluk fishers. *American Anthropologist* 104(2), 583-98.

Sosis, R. and B. J. Ruffle 2004. Ideology, religion, and the evolution of cooperation: Field experiments on Israeli Kibbutzim. *Socioeconomic Aspects of Human Behavioral Ecology* 23, 89-117.

Stein, G. J. 2002. From passive periphery to active agents: Emerging perspectives in the archaeology of interregional interaction. *American Anthropologist* 104(3), 903-16.

Thomas, P. K. 1977. *Archaeological Aspects of the Prehistoric Cultures of Western India*. Unpublished Ph.D. Dissertation, University of Poona.

Thomas, P. K. 2002. Investigations into the archaeofauna of Harappan sites in Western India. In S. Settar and R. Korisettar (eds), *Protohistory: Archaeology of the Harappan Civilization*, 409-20. Vol. II, *Indian Archaeology in Retrospect,* New Delhi, Indian Council of Historical Research and Manohar.

Thomas, P. K. and P. P. Joglekar. 1994. Holocene faunal studies in India. *Man and Environment* 19(1-2), 179-203.

Thomas, P. K. and P. P. Joglekar. 1996. Faunal remains from Balathal, Rajasthan: A preliminary report. *Man and Environment* 21(1), 91-7.

Trautmann, W. 1985. The impact of the agrarian revolution on nomadism of the Algerian Steppe. *Nomadic Peoples* 17, 23-33.

United Nations Development Programme 2002. *Rajasthan Human Development Report 2002*. Supported by the United Nations Development Programme (UNDP). Published by the Government of Rajasthan. Available online at http://data.undp.org.in/shdr/raj/rajhdr.pdf. Accessed 19 June 2008.

Vishnu-Mittre. 1969. Remains of rice and millet. In H. D. Sankalia, S. B. Deo and Z. D. Ansari (eds), *Excavations at Ahar 1961-1962*, 229-235. Pune, Deccan College.

Vishnu-Mittre. 1974. Paleobotanical evidence in India. In J. Hutchinson (ed.), *Evolutionary Studies in World Crops*, 3-30 Cambridge, Cambridge University Press.

Weber, S. 1996. Distinguishing change in the subsistence and the material records: The interplay of environment and culture. *Asian Perspectives* 35(2), 155-163.

Wienpahl, J. 1985. Turkana herds under environmental stress. *Nomadic Peoples* 17, 59-87.

Wood, J. J. 1985. Navajo livestock reduction. *Nomadic Peoples* 19, 21-31.

World Bank 2006. Rajasthan closing the development gap. Report prepared for Poverty Reduction and Economic Management Unit South Asia Region. Report No. 32585-IN. Available online at http://siteresources.worldbank.org/INDIAEXTN/Resources/Reports-Publications/366387-1140608902882/RajasthanReport_Full-Text-Feb06.pdf, accessed 19 June 2008.

5. An Insight into the Economy of the Chalcolithic People of Gilund

Debasri Dasgupta Ghosh

Introduction

The reconstruction of the economic organisation of any society requires the study of three basic economic activities: production, distribution and consumption. In addition to these, a study of economic variables such as subsistence, technology and environment is needed to understand the economic system. Towards that end, a site catchment analysis was carried out in a ten km radius around the site of Gilund, which helped in understanding all three variables of the economic system. The analysis brought to light many satellite settlements, which were set up to exploit the nearby arable and pasturelands and existing raw material resources. The analysis also revealed contact with contemporary cultures, which is quite evident from artefacts, pottery and architecture found at the site of Gilund. On the basis of these data, this paper will discuss the economic condition of Gilund throughout the Chalcolithic phase.

The ancient site of Gilund is located on the right bank of the river Banas in the Rajsamand district of Rajasthan. It is in the centre of the Mewar region and equidistant to all other Ahar culture sites. This area is characterised by a semi-arid climate and fertile black cotton soil, which is conducive to the growth of crops like wheat, barley, maize, millet, cotton and sugarcane. The average annual rainfall is 700 mm. As the agricultural production centre of Mewar, it may have participated in a system of exchange of food grains and other specialised products between Gilund and other sites of the region. The Ahar culture sites, particularly Gilund and Balathal, are located on the trade route between Gujarat and North India.

Site catchment analysis

Site catchment analysis is the study of the relationship between human needs (e.g. technological ones) and natural resources lying within the economic range or catchment area of individual archaeological sites (Higgs and Vita-Finzi 1970). A site catchment around Gilund was undertaken to identify the local resources. In addition, the analysis sought to identify the finished products manufactured at the site, the objects obtained through trade and the subsistence patterns of the people.

Based on location, size, duration and ecological conditions surrounding the site, the excavator has surmised that Gilund was the agricultural production centre of Mewar (see Shinde, this volume). The catchment area of Gilund had abundant fertile land and also area for pasture. An analysis of the data collected shows that the Chalcolithic people of Gilund fully exploited the agricultural and pastoral potentials of the catchment area.

Almost all the settlements around Gilund are located next to very productive fertile lands with potential for good crops. Agricultural products were procured by setting up camps and farmsteads throughout the ten km catchment of Gilund. In addition, excavations at Gilund yielded food processing equipments like saddle querns, mullers and pounders in large quantity, in addition to storage pits and domestic hearths made of clay starting in the Early Chalcolithic phase.

Pastoralism also played an important role in the economy of Gilund. This is evident from the fact that huge pasturelands and a number of satellite settlements were located in the catchment of Gilund. Animals such as sheep, buffalo, goat and cattle formed part of the economy of Gilund, as did hunted animals (see Landt, this volume). Hunting also seems to have played an important part at Gilund as indicated by the excavations which yielded bones of a variety of wild animals like deer, antelope, chital and blackbuck (see Landt, this volume). The river Banas, which passes at a distance of 1.20km to the north of the site, could have been an important point for animal hunting (Dasgupta 2004).

Evolution of craft specialisation and trade

While agro-pastoral activities were the mainstay of the economy, a variety of crafts were simultaneously evolving. Evidence of craft specialisation emerges from the very beginning of the Chalcolithic settlement at Gilund. Pottery production was quite important as is evident from the variety of vessels manufactured at the site. Gilund pottery is fine and well made from the beginning of the Early Chalcolithic phase onward. White painted Black and Red Ware and a variety of Red and Grey Wares were manufactured at the site. The clay in the vicinity of Gilund is very good and was presumably used to create the majority of the vessels at the site as well as various terracotta objects like beads, gamesmen, figurines, bangles, pendants, toy pots, lamps, nets, sinkers, weights and votive tanks (see Hanlon, this volume). In addition, the clay from the catchment of Gilund was also used to make mud bricks and sometimes burnt bricks. Brick manufacturing would have developed as an important craft by the Middle Chalcolithic phase when the structures were mainly built of mud bricks.

Production of lime plaster was also an important craft at Gilund. Lime plaster can be found in the structures of Gilund and in the lining of storage pits and was used profusely throughout the Chalcolithic phase. Lime plaster was most likely made at the site as the raw material for making it is abundant in the catchment area of Gilund

Microlithic tool manufacturing was another essential craft practiced by the Chalcolithic people at Gilund (see Raczek, this volume). Quite a number of microlithic tools were recovered from the Chalcolithic levels at Gilund. The presence of debitage shows that these tools were also manufactured at the site. Quartz, the main raw material, was found abundantly in the catchment of Gilund. Chert of fine quality was also used for the manufacture of tools. However, the nearest source of fine quality chert is Nathdwara. Chalcedony may also have been procured from the veins of Aravallis, located approximately 40km from the site.

A number of crafts relied on the materials brought in from other areas. For example, carnelian beads may have been manufactured at the site, indicated by the presence of debitage. Raw material was possibly obtained from Gujarat (Dasgupta 2004). Copper working seems to have been another growing craft activity. Furnaces for working copper were found in the industrial area of the site and according to the excavators, copper was worked and also could have been smelted here (see Shinde, this volume).

The importance of craft activities is also evident in the architecture. There is an industrial area located in the southern portion of GLD-2. Structure 12, a large rectangular building made of both mud and baked brick with plastered walls is located here and oriented north-south and east-west. Located above is Structure 11, which is made of mud brick and stone but with a different orientation. A large amount of vitrified clay was found in this location on the top of a succession of well made plastered floors. A large oval-shaped kiln located to the west of Structure 11 is made of mud walls. It is 4.2m in length and 80cm in width and has a north-south orientation. The kiln contained vitrified clay similar to that found in Structure 11. A second kiln to the north of structure 11 was also found. It is plastered and the walls at the base are 60 and 65cm in length (Possehl *et al.*, 2005).

The gradual development and prosperity of the site starting around 3000 BC and the gradual shift towards proto-urban lifestyle by 2500 BC is evident in the blossoming of craft activities. Construction of mud brick structures as opposed to the wattle and daub structures of the earlier period, and the replacement of circular dwellings by rectangular dwellings are evidence of the improving economic conditions. Several features show a strong Harappan influence. These include the development of fortified structures as in the citadel and lower town like appearance of Gilund, and the set of five parallel mud brick walls which are possibly a granary.

Trade contact between the Ahar people and the Gujarat Harappans is evident in the inflow of conch shell, carnelian and other semiprecious stones to Ahar sites. Beads of steatite, agate and turquoise found at the site could have been imported from the Harappans. Harappan contact also resulted in typologically similar copper objects being recovered from many of these Ahar sites like razor blades, chisels, axes, and arrowheads. The Harappans of Gujarat seem to have procured copper ingots and copper objects from the Ganeshwar region through the Ahar Banas people (see also Rizvi, this volume, for a discussion of the movement of copper).

Contact with the Harappans starting in the very early period, is evident from the presence of the Reserved Slipped Ware in the lowest levels in Gilund. The locally made Red with cream is present alongside the imported Grey with white. Also, the locally made Tan Ware is very similar to Harappan Red Ware (Shinde and Deshpande 2006).

Trade relations also existed with the Deccan Chalcolithic people in the 2nd millennium BC. This is apparent from the presence of Malwa Ware during the Mature Chalcolithic Phase in Gilund and White painted Black and Red Ware from this region. Evidence of contact with sites of the South Indian Neolithic seems probable as is evident from the similar shapes of pottery found in the Late Chalcolithic phase.

The trade network of the Ahar Banas people extended not only to the Harappans, but to the far flung regions of Afghanistan and Central Asia through the Harappans (Shinde *et al.*, 2004). The evidence comes from Gilund, where over a hundred clay seals were recovered from a bin in the northwest corner of the parallel walls. These unbaked clay seals are dated to the end of the third and the beginning of the second millennium BC and are impressed with a variety of floral motifs and the motif of the sun. As Ameri explains in this volume, seals with similar motifs are also found in the sites of Sindh and Baluchistan. The designs on the seals are also similar to the Bactria-Margiana Archaeological Complex in Central Asia and northern Afghanistan. Apart from the seals, the influence of these regions in Gilund is evident in the terracotta stepped crosses which are found as seals in the Bactria Margiana Archaeological Complex and on painted pottery in Baluchistan, especially the site of Nal (Shinde *et al.*, 2004).

Conclusion

Gilund was a flourishing regional centre based on surplus agricultural production and pastoralism. The establishment of satellite settlements in the ten km catchment of Gilund shows maximum utilisation of agro-pastoral products. They seem to have produced enough surpluses to exchange agricultural products for other trade objects like copper or semi-precious stones. This resulted in the flourishing of craft activities. They developed contacts with their near and distant neighbors. Essential goods and raw materials not available within the ten km catchment area were procured through trade. The flourishing of the Chalcolithic phase could be attributed to this flourishing trade. Also, a flourishing economy saw the development of a 'politically organised and socially stratified society' as is evident from the public structures and the lower town and citadel like structures at Gilund. The establishment of satellite settlements around Gilund also suggests the prevalence of chiefdom society, which was visible at the site of Balathal (Sinha 1998).

Bibliography

Dasgupta, D. 2004. *A Study of Site Catchment Analysis of Gilund, A Chalcolithic Settlement in the Banas Basin.* Unpublished Ph.D. Dissertation. Deccan College.

Higgs, E. S. and C. Vita-Finzi. 1970. Prehistoric economy in the Mount Carmel area of Palestine: Site catchment analysis. *Proceedings of the Prehistoric Society* 36, 1-37.

Possehl, G. L., Shinde, V. S. and M. Ameri. 2004. The Ahar Banas Complex and the BMAC. *Man and Environment* 29(2), 18-29.

Shinde, V. S. and S. S. Deshpande. 2006. Development of urbanization in the Mewar region of Rajasthan, India in the middle of third millennium BC. *Ancient Asia* I, 103-22.

Sinha, S. 1998. *Study of Chalcolithic Social Organization in Central India with Special Reference to Balathal.* Unpublished M.A. Dissertation, Deccan College.

6. Contextualising Gilund: A Comparative Analysis of Technology

Teresa P. Raczek

In the third and second millennia BC, lithic production was an important part of the technological repertoire of the inhabitants of the Mewar Plain in northwest India. Lithic use occurred on a daily basis for many people, and the production of lithics does not appear to have been a specialised activity in this region. Instead, it appears that many people produced most, if not all, of their own lithic tools. Thousands of these lithics were recently found at the site of Gilund during excavations. Because lithic technologies were also employed by the inhabitants of the nearby site of Bagor, a detailed study of the core and blade production techniques used at both sites was undertaken. The comparative analysis sought to identify common techniques used at these sites and to ascertain whether the inhabitants shared a similar skill set. Using a comparative approach illustrates the links between sites in the ancient past and permits the observation of daily life on a regional level.

The study of lithics is of great importance for understanding broader questions about society. Lithic assemblages are created and shaped by a social context that includes factors such as mobility, subsistence practices, craft activities and other aspects of daily life. However, environmental factors such as proximity of stone raw materials and quality of local stone also affect assemblages. Thus, variation among lithic assemblages from different sites index technological trends and social practices as well as environmental conditions.

Lithic cores are particularly interesting because they leave signatures that reflect the way they were produced. As a result, the study of cores is highly useful for tracking production methodologies. As there are multiple ways of producing blade cores, similarities in core production processes between different communities indicate that skills and knowledge may have been shared.

In many ways, blade production is a technological tradition and an acquired skill. Basic knapping can be learned quickly, but blade core preparation takes more training and practice. However, the skill is not so difficult that it can only be mastered by full time specialists. Although there are many ways to manufacture blades, blade removal techniques are frequently shared by members of a community and tend to be passed down between generations. However, lithic production is not necessarily a conservative technology; it does not resist change, but often shifts with changes in raw material access, mobility levels and intended use, among other factors.

Previous studies of South Asian core technologies have provided great insight into blade manufacturing techniques. For example, the use of pressure debitage has been identified in collections from multiple Holocene sites in South Asia including Bagor (Inizan and Lechevallier 1985, 1990, 1995; Lechevallier 2003; Pelegrin 1994). Pressure debitage is a sophisticated blade production technique that allows for precision in blade removals. At Bagor, Marie Inizan and Monique Lechevalier identify the presence of pressure debitage that was 'most probably done by the hand' (Inizan and Lechevallier 1995, 18). At some sites, it appears that a copper tipped instrument was used to remove blades (Anderson-Gerfaud et al., 1989; Inizan et al., 1994; Méry et al., 2007). The use of copper-tipped punches has multiple ramifications, not the least of which is the identification of copper at sites where copper artefacts may not have been retrieved during excavation. The use of copper to produce stone tools also delightfully upends standard conceptions of the evolution of technology.

Some researchers have noted that cores recovered from microlithic sites in Rajasthan and Gujarat appear to be somewhat unique (Ajithprasad 2002; Allchin and Allchin 1974; Hooja and Kumar 1997). P. Ajithprasad has mentioned that a unique core type can be found throughout Gujarat from sites dated to the fifth millennium BC and later and suggests that these cores are prepared in an unusual way. For example, the blade cores from pre-ceramic levels of Pithad, a site dated only through ceramic sequences, seem to have been made from flakes, as opposed to raw nodules (Ajithprasad 1992 in Sonawane 2002).

Gilund and its Neighbors

The sites included in this analysis were inhabited in the third and second millennia BC in the Mewar Plain of southeastern Rajasthan. At that time, the region was inhabited by a diverse range of communities who engaged in a spectrum of mobility and subsistence strategies. Over 100 permanent agro-pastoral settlements of the Ahar-Banas complex have been identified through survey in southeastern Rajasthan (Hooja 1988; Misra 1967). In addition to Gilund, four of these sites have been excavated in Rajasthan (Meena and Tripathi 2000, 2001-2002; Misra 1997; Misra et al., 1995; Misra et al., 1997; Mohanty et al., 2000; Sankalia et al., 1969). Excavated sites in Madhya Pradesh with Ahar-Banas material include Chichali (Mittra and Shivananda 2000), Kayatha (Ansari and Dhavalikar 1973; Wakankar 1969), Eran (Pandey 1982; Singh 1967a, b), Navdatoli (Sankalia et *al.*, 1958; Sankalia *et al.*, 1971) and Nagda (Banerjee 1986).

Gilund is a very large agro-pastoral settlement located in the middle of the Mewar Plain. It was occupied from approximately 3000 BC through 1700 BC, with continued settlement well into historic periods. Because of its location and size, the site is frequently considered to be a political and economic centre of the Ahar-Banas cultural complex (see Shinde this volume). The original excavations by B. B. Lal (IAR 1959-60) revealed the presence of a large monumental building in the form of a series of connected parallel-mudbrick walls. Recent excavations by Vasant Shinde of Deccan College and Gregory L. Possehl of the University of Pennsylvania also found evidence for workshops with pyrotechnic features, houses and artefacts that point to local and long-distance exchange throughout the third and second millenniums BC (Shinde and Possehl 2005, Shinde *et al.*, 2005).

In addition to sites with Ahar-Banas cultural material, hundreds of lithic scatters have been located in this region through survey. The site of Bagor is one of these (IAR 1967-68, 1968-69, 1969-70; Misra 1973, 1982). Originally excavated by V. N. Misra in the late 1960s, Bagor differs from Ahar-Banas sites because it largely consists of a microlithic scatter, although other materials were recovered during the excavations. The Phase I occupation dates from 5500 to 2800 BC while the Phase II occupation dates from 2800 to 600 BC (Misra 1973). It is the Phase II occupation that overlaps with most of the Ahar-Banas sites. In the Phase II layers, the excavators found pottery with affinities to the ceramic assemblages of the Ahar-Banas as well as stone and carnelian beads, a copper spearhead, a copper awl and three copper arrowheads (Misra 1970, 1973). These finds suggest that the inhabitants of Bagor had an as yet undefined relationship with the inhabitants of other settlements on the Mewar Plain and beyond.

Researchers collected far more lithics at both Gilund and Bagor than at other excavated sites in the region. Few lithics were recovered from the excavations at Ahar, although thousands of chipped quartz pieces were observed (Ansari 1969). Similarly, few lithics were recovered from the Balathal excavations. The published reports from Ojiyana do not mention lithic remains. However, hundreds of small lithics were personally observed in multiple concentrations on the surface and in the erosion channels of the site of Purani Marmi, the nearest of the excavated sites to Gilund. Even correcting for different occupational periods, the variable use of stone at these sites is quite interesting. One of the factors influencing this observed difference may be the location of excavation trenches and perhaps excavation methods[1]. However, other factors must be considered including the availability of local stone material and the availability of alternative tool materials such as copper. In addition, the types of activities and tasks performed at each site contributed to differences in stone tool use. Although the densities of lithics at these sites vary greatly, the lithic technology superficially appears to be very similar. That is, lithic technologies observed at Ahar and Marmi include blade and microlithic technology, as well as simple flake production. Multiple raw materials were used at both sites, especially locally available quartz. As will be shown below, these general descriptions match the collections from Gilund and Bagor.

Comparing Gilund and Bagor is a useful exercise because these sites are very different and the inhabitants utilised different settlement and subsistence strategies. Gilund was a permanent settlement and Bagor was, for the most part, a temporary habitation. The inhabitants of Gilund relied mainly upon domesticated plants and animals that they supplemented with some wild plant and animal resources, while those of Bagor emphasised pastoralism which they supplemented with wild animals and both wild and domesticated plants (Landt, this volume; Kashyap 2006; Thomas 1975, 1977). I do not wish to essentialise either site or the differences between them; however, it is important to consider these differences when examining the technology employed at each site. Technology is culturally embedded; as a result, differences in daily routines and practices become manifest in technological objects such as stone tools.

Analysis of Gilund and Bagor Lithics: Methods

This study examined nearly 25,000 lithics from the new Gilund excavations which were conducted by a joint team from Deccan College and the University of Pennsylvania from 1999-2005. Although lithics were encountered in almost all areas of the site, most were concentrated on the eastern side of GLD-2, just south of the large parallel walled structure. Many of these were found in relation to three mud-brick wall segments that were encountered approximately one meter below current ground surface. Additional lithics were found between and under the parallel walls. Lower densities of lithics were identified in the upper levels of GLD-2, which were occupied in later periods. Although thousands of lithics were recovered, the samples included in this study were limited to lithics from excellent depositional contexts that were contemporaneous to other sites in the region. As a result, 2830 lithics were included in the primary study sample.

In addition to the Gilund lithics, over 10,000 specimens from the new Bagor excavations conducted by Deccan College in 2001 were examined using the same methods. Both the Gilund and Bagor excavations used the same methodologies including screening of all soil through fine-mesh screens and collection of all visible chipped stone. The study samples selected from the Bagor excavations came from Layers 3 and 4 of Trench 1A, the index trench, which was 5m x 5m in extent. A total of 1564 lithics were selected for comparison with Gilund in the primary study sample. Because the soil volumes excavated from each site varied greatly, comparisons of raw numbers between the sites should be avoided.

---

[1] The use of regular screening with fine mesh screens potentially allows excavators to recover more lithics.

During analysis, the lithics were divided into two groups: the primary study sample and the secondary study sample. Artefacts in the primary study sample consisted of all complete and proximal pieces, along with the medial and distal pieces of all tools and worked pieces. Artefacts in the secondary study sample included all non-tool, non-worked medial and distal pieces and shatter (chips and chunks). Artefacts in the primary study sample were studied and recorded individually, while artefacts in the secondary study sample were grouped by type and raw material, counted and weighed. Lithics were assigned a type based on a modified version of Misra's typology (Misra 1973). In addition, both metric and non-metric attributes, including raw material attributes, were recorded for the primary study sample. In all, over four dozen points of data were collected in order to compare multiple attributes. Using this abundant data I have been able to address questions about landscape usage, technological practices and skill sets. In addition, I have been able to describe the technological organisation of each site and to pinpoint the specific differences between the collections of these sites. A full description of all of the analyses and their results can be found in Raczek (2007) and the forthcoming monograph on the Gilund excavations. The results presented here come from the primary study sample and emphasise a detailed analysis of cores.

Analysis of Gilund Lithics: Results

The full assemblage

The primary study sample at Gilund is mainly comprised of flakes and blades with very few formal tools, or backed pieces. In addition, approximately half of all analysed lithics were categorised as shatter, or chips and chunks. This is due in part to the high use of quartz, which fractures considerably when worked. Bagor has significantly more tools than Gilund, but not significantly more blades compared to flakes. Bagor has comparatively more microburins and fewer burins than Gilund. Overall, the assemblage from Gilund is slightly more expedient than that of Bagor, which is slightly more formal. Expedient products, like flakes, can be used for immediate cutting needs without being hafted. Formal products, like geometric tools, are carefully designed for use in hafted composite tools, like scythes and arrows. Emphasis on either expedient or formal technologies may indicate differences in mobility levels, activities performed regularly, or raw material use (Andrefsky 1994; Bamforth 1991; Brantingham *et al.*, 2000; Close 1996; Cowan 1999; Kuhn 1994; Odell 1996, 1998; Parry and Kelly 1987; Shott 1986; Wallace and Shea 2006).

Quartz is plentiful in the areas near both sites, so it is not surprising that the majority of both assemblages were made of this local material. Smaller percentages of lithics were made of cherts, chalcedony and a few other materials. However, there is also a significant difference between Gilund and Bagor with respect to the use of quartz and non-quartz materials. Gilund uses more quartz than Bagor. Most chert and chalcedony deposits are located at some distance from the sites of Gilund and Bagor, near the current border with Madhya Pradesh (Khanna 1993; Raczek 2010). However, some lower quality chert can be found in the Banas River, near Gilund. The significant difference of raw material use between these two sites may indicate that the inhabitants of Bagor had greater access to chert sources than those of Gilund. This greater access to exotic raw materials might point to higher mobility levels among the inhabitants of Bagor, compared to Gilund.

In sum, the differences between these two assemblages are very limited. While there is some variation in the distribution of types, many of the differences lie within the distribution of raw materials. The root of these differences may lie in varying activities performed at each site and variation in mobility practices, among other factors.

The Cores

This core analysis was undertaken in order to identify the range of core preparation and blade removal techniques utilised at Gilund and Bagor, and to determine whether the knappers at these two sites used the same techniques. Recorded attributes presented here include core type (i.e. blade or flake), raw material, blade removal pattern, initiation and platform count. A total of 162 cores from Gilund and 89 cores from Bagor were selected for intensive study.

		Bagor		Gilund	
		N	%	N	%
Blade cores	Chalcedony	1	1.3%	0	0.0%
	Chert	26	33.8%	5	4.7%
	Quartz	50	64.9%	102	95.3%
BLADE CORES TOTAL		77	100.0%	107	100.0%
Flake cores	Quartz	12	100.0%	55	100.0%
FLAKE CORES TOTAL		12	100.0%	55	100.0%
TOTAL		89		162	

Figure 6.1 Core types by raw material and site

Core Type

Cores were categorised as either blade cores or flake cores. Cores with both blade and flake scars were categorised as blade cores. Both sites had a preponderance of blade cores, as compared to flake cores (see Figure 6.1 Core types by raw material and site). However, Gilund had significantly fewer blade cores (compared to flake cores) than Bagor (66.0% versus 86.5%), which parallels a similar finding of the difference between Gilund and Bagor regarding flakes and blades. The emphasis on flake cores at Gilund may indicate a preference for expedient technologies over more formal ones.

Raw Material

The majority of cores at both sites were made of quartz (see Figure 6.1). Overall, there are few chalcedony cores, and none of the chalcedony blade cores from Gilund fell within the study sample. When comparing non-quartz to quartz cores, Gilund had significantly more quartz cores than Bagor. This difference mirrors differentiation found among the non-core lithics. A variety of cherts were also identified among the cores of both sites, although Bagor had more chert blade cores.

Blade removal pattern

Multiple blade removal patterns were observed and recorded. In this analysis, cores were divided into three general categories: sliced, rotated and flexible. Cores can be sliced from front to back, with one row of blades removed behind the other, in a similar way to slicing bread. Wedge cores are examples of this kind of core. Cores can also be rotated in a circular fashion as blades are removed so that blades are removed in sequence around the core. Prismatic, pyramid, cylinder and bullet cores are examples of these types of cores. Finally, some cores have been worked in multiple opportunistic or flexible ways without systematic slicing or rotating. These cores include block or amorphous cores. It should be cautioned that over the life of the core, several removal techniques may have been used. As a result, the final core as seen by archaeologists represents the final stage of production, and may not reflect what the core looked like in its early stages. However, a large enough sample includes a range of cores that represent a variety of stages of use.

Both sites have a majority of cores that were worked from front to back (Bagor 58.8%, Gilund 50.9%), followed by flexible cores (Bagor 38.8%, Gilund 40.4%). Neither site has many rotated cores (Bagor 2.4%, Gilund 8.7%). This indicates that although both Gilund and Bagor used a variety of blade removal patterns, they rarely utilised a rotating system. There is no significant difference in distribution between the two sites when considering these three categories of core shape. The blade removal strategies employed by Gilund and Bagor appear to be very similar.

Initiation

In an effort to understand how blade cores were prepared and worked at each site, each core was examined for evidence of the technique employed to remove the first blade. In blade cores there are typically three types of initial blades: crested ridges, burin spalls and natural ridges. For most cores in the study sample, multiple blade scars were present and the initial blade scar was no longer distinguishable. As a result, it was not possible to determine how the first blade was initiated. For 25% of the Bagor collection (N=18) and 31% of the Gilund collection (N=33), the initial blade scar remained and it was possible to identify how the first blade was removed.

In some cases, the first removal resembled a burin blow, which created two additional ridges that allowed the knapper to continue his or her work. Burin-blow initiations have been observed in multiple contexts outside of South Asia (Barton et al., 1996; Chazan 2001; Coinman and Clausen 2000; Crabtree 1968; Parry 1994). About 23% of Gilund blade cores and 26% of Bagor blade cores have a burin initiation. There is no significant difference in the use of this technique.

Platform Count

At both sites, blade cores had three or fewer platforms (see Figure 6.2, Blade core platform count). Most blade cores at both sites had only one platform (Bagor: N=60, 82.2%; Gilund N=78, 72.9%). Blade cores with more than one platform were worked initially on one face; then the core was turned and more blades were removed from a new platform. Occasionally the blade scars intersected, leaving a residual crested ridge. However, in most cases, this ridge was at an awkward angle to any other potential platform and could not easily have been used as an initiating ridge. The difference in platform numbers between Gilund and Bagor is not significant. This indicates that the inhabitants of Gilund and Bagor used similar strategies with regard to platform rejuvenation.

Platform count	Bagor		Gilund	
	N	%	N	%
1	60	82.2%	78	72.9%
2	12	16.4%	27	25.2%
3	1	1.4%	2	1.9%
TOTAL	73	100.0%	107	100.0%

Figure 6.2 Blade core platform count

Discussion

Lithic cores are the waste products discarded after the production of useful flakes and blades. As such, they bear scars that tell the story of their use and the techniques used in the production of flakes and blades. Factors that affect the final appearance of a core at discard include factors like raw material, intensity of use, initiation technique, blade removal sequence and the number of platforms used.

It is commonly accepted that most blade cores in the 2nd and 3rd millenniums BC in South Asia were started with a crested ridge technique (Sankalia 1982; Subbarao 1955). In this technique, an artificial ridge is created by removing a series of small flakes in a line. Then, the top of the ridge is struck, in this case through pressure, to remove the first blade. This technique is common in the Indus and in the Deccan. However, an alternative to the crested ridge is the use of a burin-blow. For burination to be possible, an edge from previous flaking must be available. Large, fat flakes with fresh edges can be easily burinated and converted into a bladelet core. No crested ridge is needed because a flake has usable ridges on the two side edges and on the bottom edge. This system is found in many places throughout the world including the Near East, North America and Mesoamerica (Barton et al., 1996; Chazan 2001; Crabtree 1968; Parry 1994). Archaeologists who have studied blade cores that begin with burins have noted that it is not possible to distinguish between a burin spall and an initial blade made with a burin blow (Barton et al., 1996). In addition, a blade core with only a single blade removed with this technique will look exactly like a burin. This may explain the high numbers of burins identified in the Gilund collection.

Using a burin-like initiation is a fast technique. However, there are drawbacks to using it. First, it is more difficult to make longer narrow blades. Typically, crested ridges are used when producing long narrow blades. This may explain why crested ridges were used to produce Harappan blades, since those blades tend to be long. However, the blades and cores of Rajasthan appear to be among the smallest of South Asia, which means that a burin blow would have been sufficient for initiation. Second, this technique is easy to use on material that has natural ridges, but more difficult to use on material without ridges like small rounded river nodules. Most blade cores in the Deccan are made from such material which might explain the preference for crested ridges in that location. Finally, it has been suggested that it is more 'wasteful' to create the initial blade without a crested ridge (Arnold 1987, 228). However, at Gilund and Bagor, quartz was plentiful, so conservation and prevention of waste may not have been important. At these sites, it seems that the combination of abundant material with natural ridges and a desire for shorter blades made the use of a burinated initiation both feasible and preferred.

In addition to a unique blade initiation technique, Gilund cores are also interesting because of the way that they were worked after the first blade was removed. Most of the cores at Gilund are not cylindrical, but appear to have been worked on one face, with the blades removed like slices of bread, moving from front to back. While the cores are not true wedge cores in that they do not begin as bifaces, they are worked in a similar way to wedge cores found throughout Asia. Like Gilund, the cores at Bagor also appear to have been sliced more often than rotated. Rotated cores usually have one platform from which all blades are removed. Since the core is rotated as blades are removed, there is no need to begin a second platform. When the platform becomes dull or damaged, it is removed with a side blow, and the resulting core tab is discarded, leaving a fresh platform in the same location as the original platform. The cores from Gilund, however, frequently have multiple platforms. After a number of blades have been removed, the entire core is repositioned and a new face is selected for blade removals, so they are shaped very differently.

Conclusion

Unlike other excavated Ahar-Banas sites, vast quantities of lithics were recovered at Gilund, mostly in, under and around the parallel walls. The Gilund assemblage varies somewhat from the assemblage from Bagor in that it is more expediently made and less formal than the Bagor assemblage. However, the core production techniques used at both sites are very similar. Both sites rely heavily on the use of a burin blow to initiate blade production in contrast to sites in the Indus and Deccan where the use of the crested ridge is more common. In addition, there is evidence from both sites that in many cases, blades were removed from cores like slices of bread, instead of in a spiral, rotating fashion. Finally, the use of multiple platforms was common in both collections.

The core production technology appears to be quite similar between these sites and may indicate the sharing of technological knowledge or traditional techniques. It is possible that emphasis on a burinated initiation followed by a sliced blade removal pattern is local to this region. However, as core attributes are rarely recorded for South Asian lithics, it is not possible to say how common the blade removal techniques of Gilund and Bagor are.

Although a similar core production strategy was used, the overall lithic assemblages at Gilund and Bagor differ somewhat. Differences occur in the emphasis on flakes and flake products at Gilund, as opposed to blades and blade products as well as the emphasis on the use of local materials at Gilund. These differences may indicate variations in practices related to mobility, subsistence strategies and other activities.

Returning to the question of the relationship between Gilund and its neighbors, this research extends and supports previous research that has identified links between Gilund and other sites in the region as well as regions in all four directions. Such links have been found in other material classes such as pottery (see Dasgupta, this volume), bull figurines (see Hanlon, this volume), seals and seal impressions (Ameri this volume) and in raw materials like shell (Landt, this volume) and stone (Raczek 2007). Previous research also found a connection between Ahar-Banas sites and Bagor in the form of copper arrowheads and Black and Red ware. Although it is not possible at this time to compare the Gilund lithics to those from all other Ahar-Banas sites, a comparison with Bagor has proved to be quite fruitful. The analysis of lithics provides further evidence for previously recognised connections by identifying the use of a similar technological skill set at both sites. This finding may add to the idea that there was a sustained contact and shared history between the occupants of the various sites in the region. Although Gilund and Bagor appear to be quite different because of their subsistence and mobility patterns, evidence suggests that some sustained relationship existed between them.

Acknowledgements

I am grateful to Drs V. Shinde and G. L. Possehl for inviting me to join them in the excavations at Gilund and for permission to analyse the Gilund and Bagor material. I also thank the Archaeological Survey of India for permission to do this work. Dr V. N. Misra provided crucial guidance at key moments in the analysis phase. Funding was provided by the William J. Fulbright Foundation and the Zwicker Fellowship at the University of Pennsylvania. Logistical assistance was provided by the American Institute for Indian Studies and the United States Educational Foundation in India.

Bibliography

Ajithprasad, P. 2002. The Mesolithic culture in the Orsang Valley, Gujarat. In Misra, V. N. and J. N. Pal (eds), *Mesolithic India*, 154-89. Allahabad, Department of Ancient History, Culture and Archaeology, University of Allahabad.

Allchin, F. R. and B. Allchin. 1974. The relationship of Neolithic and later settled communities with those of Late Stone Age hunters and gatherers in peninsular India. In Sharma, R. S. and V. Jha (eds), *Indian Society: Historical Probings in Memory of D. D. Kosambi*, 45-66. New Delhi, People's Publishing House.

Anderson-Gerfaud, P., M. -L. Inizan, M. Lechevallier, J. Pelegrin and M. Pernot. 1989. Des lames de silex dans un atelier de potier Harappéen: Interaction de domaines techniques. *Comptes Rendus de L'Académie des Sciences - Serie II* 308, 443-9.

Andrefsky, W. J. 1994. Raw-material availability and the organization of technology. *American Antiquity* 59(1), 21-35.

Ansari, Z. D. 1969. Lithic flake tools. In Sankalia, H. D., S. B. Deo and Z. D. Ansari (eds), *Excavations at Ahar (Tambavati)*, 15-7. Pune, Deccan College Postgraduate and Research Institute.

Ansari, Z. D. and M. K. Dhavalikar. 1973. *Excavations at Kayatha*. Pune, Deccan College.

Archaeological Survey of India
1959-60. Excavations at Gilund. *Indian Archaeology: A Review* (IAR), 41-6.
1967-68. Excavations at Bagor. *Indian Archaeology: A Review* (IAR), 41-2.
1968-69. Excavations at Bagor. *Indian Archaeology: A Review* (IAR), 26-8.
1969-70. Excavations at Bagor. *Indian Archaeology: A Review* (IAR), 32-3.

Arnold, J. M. 1987. Technology and economy: Microblade core production from the Channel Islands. In Johnson, J. K. and C. A. Morrow (eds), *The Organization of Core Technology*, 207-38. Boulder and London, Westview.

Bamforth, D. B. 1991. Technological organization and hunter-gatherer land use: A California example. *American Antiquity* 56(2), 216-34.

Banerjee, N. R. 1986. *Nagda: 1955-57*. New Delhi, Archaeological Survey of India, Government of India.

Barton, C. M., D. I. Olszewski and N. R. Coinman. 1996. Beyond the graver: Reconsidering burin function. *Journal of Field Archaeology* 23(1), 111-25.

Brantingham, P. J., J. W. Olsen, J. A. Rech and A. I. Krivoshapkin. 2000. Raw material quality and prepared core technologies in northeast Asia. *Journal of Archaeological Science* 27(3), 255-71.

Chazan, M. 2001. Bladelet production in the Aurignacian of la Ferrassie (Dordogne, France). *Lithic Technology* 26(1), 16-28.

Close, A. E. 1996. Carry that weight: The use and transportation of stone tools. *Current Anthropology* 37(3), 545-53.

Coinman, N. R. and T. G. Clausen 2000. Burins revisited: A re-examination of the burins from Ain al-Buhira (WHS 618). In Coinman, N. R. (ed.), *The Archaeology of the Wadi al-Hasa, West-Central Jordan*, 183-94. Phoenix, Arizona Board of Regents.

Cowan, F. L. 1999. Making sense of flake scatters: Lithic technological strategies and mobility. *American Antiquity* 64(4), 593-607.

Crabtree, D. 1968. Mesoamerican polyhedral cores and prismatic blades. *American Antiquity* 33 (4), 446-78.

Hooja, R. 1988. *The Ahar Culture and Beyond: Settlements and Frontiers of 'Mesolithic' and Early Agricultural Sites in South-eastern Rajasthan, c. 3rd-2nd Millennia B.C.* British Archaeological Reports International Series 412, Oxford, British Archaeological Reports.

Hooja, R. and V. Kumar. 1997. Aspects of the early copper age in Rajasthan. In Allchin, R. and B. Allchin (eds), *South Asian Archaeology 1995: Proceedings of the 13th Conference of the European Association of South Asian Archaeologists, Cambridge, 5-9 July, 1995*, 323-35. New Delhi, Ancient India and Iran Trust.

Inizan, M. -L. and M. Lechevallier. 1985. La taille du silex par pression a Mehrgarh, Pakistan: La tombe d'un tailleur. *Paleorient* 11(1), 111-8.

Inizan, M. -L. and M. Lechevallier. 1990. A techno-economic approach to lithics: Some examples of blade pressure debitage in the Indo-Pakistani subcontinent. In Taddei, M. (ed.), *South Asian Archaeology 1987*, 43-59. Rome, Istituto Italiano per il Medio ed Estremo Oriente, Serie Orientale Roma, 66(1).

Inizan, M. -L. and M. Lechevallier. 1995. Pressure debitage and heat treatment in the microlithic assemblage of Bagor, northwest India. *Man and Environment* 20 (2), 17-22.

Inizan, M. -L., M. Lechevallier and J. Pelegrin. 1994. The use of metal in the lithics of Sheri Khan Tarakai,

Pakistan: Evidence provided by the technical approach of pressure debitage. In Parpola, A. and P. Koskikallio (eds), *South Asian Archaeology 1993*, 245-56. Helsinki, Annales Academiae Scientiarum Fennicae, Ser. B, Vol. 271.

Kashyap, A. 2006. *Use-Wear and Starch Grain Analysis: An Integrated Approach to Understanding the Transition from Hunting and Gathering to Food Production at Bagor, Rajasthan, India*. Unpublished Ph.D. Dissertation. Michigan State University.

Khanna, G. S. 1993. Patterns of mobility in the Mesolithic of Rajasthan. *Man and Environment* 18(1), 49-55.

Kuhn, S. L. 1994. A formal approach to the design and assembly of mobile toolkits. *American Antiquity* 59(3), 426-42.

Lechevallier, M. 2003. *L'industrie Lithique de Mehrgarh: Fouilles 1974-1985*. Paris, Éditions Recherche sur les Civilisations.

Meena, B. R. and A. Tripathi. 2000. Excavation at Ojiyana. *Puratattva* 30, 67-73.

Meena, B. R. and A. Tripathi. 2001-2002. Excavations at Ojiyana: A unique copper age site in Aravalli. *Pragdhara* 12, 45-66.

Méry, S., P. Anderson, M. -L. Inizan, M. Lechevallier and J. Pelegrin. 2007. A pottery workshop with flint tools on blades knapped with copper at Naushro (Indus Civilization, ca. 2500 BC). *Journal of Archaeological Science* 34, 1098-116.

Misra, V. N. 1967. *Pre- and Proto-history of the Berach Basin South Rajasthan*. Pune, Deccan College Postgraduate and Research Institute.

Misra, V. N. 1970. Cultural significance of three copper arrow-heads from Rajasthan India. *Journal of Near Eastern Studies* 29(4), 221-31.

Misra, V. N. 1973. Bagor: A late Mesolithic settlement in north-west India. *World Archaeology* 5(1), 92-100.

Misra, V. N. 1982. Bagor: The archaeological setting. In Lukacs, J. R., V. N. Misra and K. A. R. Kennedy (eds), *Bagor and Tilwara: Late Mesolithic Cultures of Northwest India, Volume I: The Human Skeletal Remains*, 9-20. Pune, Deccan College Postgraduate and Research Institute.

Misra, V. N. 1997. Balathal: A Chalcolithic settlement in Mewar, Rajasthan, India: Results of the first three season's excavation. *South Asian Studies* 13, 251-73.

Misra, V. N., V. Shinde, R. K. Mohanty, L. Pandey and J. Kharakwal. 1997. Excavations at Balathal, Udaipur District, Rajasthan (1995-97), with special reference to Chalcolithic architecture. *Man and Environment* 22(2), 35-60.

Misra, V. N., V. Shinde, R.K. Mohanty, K. Dalal, A. Mishra, L. Pandey and J. Kharakwal. 1995. The excavations at Balathal: Their contribution to the Chalcolithic and Iron Age cultures of Mewar. *Man and Environment* 20(1), 57-80.

Mittra, S. K. and V. Shivananda. 2000. Chalcolithic settlements at Chichali. *Puratattva* 30, 45-9.

Mohanty, R. K., A. Mishra, P. Joglekar, P. K. Thomas, J. Kharakwal and T. Panda. 2000. Purani Marmi: A Late Ahar culture settlement in Chittaurgarh District, Rajasthan. *Puratattva* 30, 132-41.

Odell, G. H. 1996. Economizing behavior and the concept of 'curation'. In Odell, G. H. (ed.), *Stone Tools: Theoretical Insights into Human Prehistory*, 51-80. New York and London, Plenum Press.

Odell, G. H. 1998. Investigating correlates of sedentism and domestication in prehistoric North America. *American Antiquity* 63, 553-71.

Pandey, S. K. 1982. Chalcolithic Eran and its chronology. In Sharma, R. K. (ed.), *Indian Archaeology: New Perspectives*, 249-56. Delhi, Agam Kala Prakashan.

Parry, W. J. 1994. Prismatic blade technologies in North America. In Carr, P. J. (ed.), *The Organization of North American Prehistoric Chipped Stone Tool Technologies*, 87-98. Ann Arbor, International Monographs in Prehistory.

Parry, W. J. and R. L. Kelly. 1987. Expedient core technology and sedentism. In Johnson, J. K. and C. A. Morrow (eds), *The Organization of Core Technology*, 285-304. Boulder, Westview Press.

Pelegrin, J. 1994. Lithic technology in Harappan times. In Parpola, A. and P. Koskikallio (eds), *South Asian Archaeology 1993*, 587-98. Annales Academiae Scientiarum Fennicae, Series B, Volume 271, 2 Vols. Helsinki.

Raczek, T. P. 2007. *Shared Histories: Technology and Community at Gilund and Bagor, Rajasthan, India (c. 3000-1700 BC)*. Unpublished Ph.D. Dissertation. University of Pennsylvania.

Raczek, T. P. 2010. In the context of copper: Indian lithics in the third millennium BC. In B. V. Eriksen (ed.), *Lithic Technology in Metal Using Societies*, 231-45. Proceedings of a UISPP Workshop, Lisbon, September 2006. Højbjerg: Jutland Archaeological Society.

Sankalia, H. D. 1982. *Stone Age Tools: Their Techniques, Names and Probable Functions*. Pune, Deccan College Postgraduate and Research Institute.

Sankalia, H. D., B. Subbarao and S. B. Deo. 1958. *The Excavations at Maheshwar and Navdatoli 1952-53*. Publication No. 1. Pune/Baroda, Deccan College Postgraduate and Research Institute/Maharaja Sayajiro University.

Sankalia, H. D., S. B. Deo and Z. D. Ansari. 1969. *Excavations at Ahar (Tambavati)*. Pune, Deccan College Post-graduate and Research Institute.

Sankalia, H. D., S. B. Deo and Z. D. Ansari. 1971. *Chalcolithic Navdatoli: The Excavations at Navdatoli 1957-59*. Publication No. 2. Pune/Baroda, Deccan College Postgraduate and Research Institute/Maharaja Sayajiro University.

Shinde, V. and G. L. Possehl. 2005. A report on the excavations at Gilund, 1999-2001. In Jarrige, C. and V. Lefèvre (eds), *South Asian Archaeology 2001*, 293-302. Paris, Éditions Recherche sur les Civilisations.

Shinde, V., G. L. Possehl and M. Ameri. 2005. Excavations at Gilund 2001-2003: The seal impressions and other finds. In Franke-Vogt, U. and H. -J. Weisshar (eds), *South Asian Archaeology 2003*, 155-65. Aachen, Linden Soft.

Shott, M. J. 1986. Technological organization and settlement mobility: An ethnographic examination. *Journal of Anthropological Research* 42(1), 15-51.

Singh, U. V. 1967a. Eran: A Chalcolithic settlement. *Bulletin of the Department of Ancient Indian History and Archaeology* 1, 29-30.

Singh, U. V. 1967b. Further excavations at Eran. *Journal of the Madhya Pradesh Itihasa Parishad* 5, 19-27.

Sonawane, V. H. 2002. Post-urban Harappan culture in Gujarat. In Settar, S. and R. Korisettar (eds), *Protohistory: Archaeology of the Harappan Civilization*, 159-72. New Delhi, Indian Council of Historical Research and Manohar.

Subbarao, B. 1955. Chalcolithic blade industry of Maheshwar (Central India) and a note on the history of the technique. *Bulletin of the Deccan College Post-graduate and Research Institute* 17, 126-49.

Thomas, P. K. 1975. The role of animals in the food economy of the Mesolithic culture of western and central India. In Clason, A. T. (ed.), *Archaeozoological Studies*, 322-28. Amsterdam, North-Holland.

Thomas, P. K. 1977. *Archaeozoological Aspects of the Prehistoric Cultures of Western India.* Unpublished Ph.D. Dissertation. Deccan College.

Wakankar, V. S. 1969. Kayatha excavation. *Ujjain: Vikram University Journal.* Special Number 1-52.

Wallace, I. J. and J. Shea. 2006. Mobility patterns and core technologies in the Middle Paleolithic of the Levant. *Journal of Archaeological Science* 33, 1293-309.

7. Middle Asian Interconnections at the Turn of the Second Millennium BC: Locating the Foreign Elements in the Gilund Seals and Seal Impressions

Marta Ameri

The analysis of contacts and interactions between geographically distant cultures has always played an important role in archaeological research. In fact, when the Harappan cities were first discovered, it was the presence of Harappan type artefacts in well dated contexts in Mesopotamia that made the dating of the Indus Civilization possible. Since then, relations between the Indus Valley and the lands to the west have been a major focus of South Asian archaeology. In recent years, the discovery of seals and seal impressions that strongly resemble material known from Iran and Central Asia at sites in western India has added an interesting piece to the puzzle. Materials of this type are well documented at Indus sites and throughout Iran and Western Asia. Their discovery at the Ahar-Banas site of Gilund suggests that the interaction networks that brought them there in fact spread much farther than was previously believed. This article will examine several of the most distinctive seal amulets and seals impressed on sealings found at Gilund in an attempt to place them within the wider contexts of Middle Asian iconographies of the third to second millennia BC.

The initial reaction to the seals and seal amulets found at Gilund related them to material, particularly seals, excavated at sites belonging to the Bactria Margiana Archaeological Complex (BMAC) and at sites as far afield as Iran, Mesopotamia and the Gulf (Possehl *et al.*, 2004; Shinde *et al.*, 2005). These seals, as well as certain types of weapons and stone vessels, have at times been interpreted as evidence of a BMAC expansion (Hiebert and Lamberg-Karlovsky 1992) or even as evidence of the Aryan invasion documented in the *Rgveda* (Parpola 2006) at the beginning of the second millennium BC. However, a more thorough examination suggests that the iconography found on the seals and seal amulets from Gilund was in fact in existence throughout Middle Asia, and possibly made its way to India, as early as the middle of the third millennium BC.

The glyptic material from Gilund can be divided into two classes—the sealings and the seal amulets. The majority of the sealings were found in a large structure dated to the Middle Ahar-Banas period that consists of at least five parallel walls and a number of subsidiary structures located on the west side of mound GLD-2 (Figure 7.1). Most were found in a meticulously plastered bin placed in the northwest corner of one of the subsidiary rooms associated with the parallel wall structure. In addition to the plaster lining, the bin had a brick coping around its top edge and two small brick walls, one on its south side and one on the north, which may have functioned either

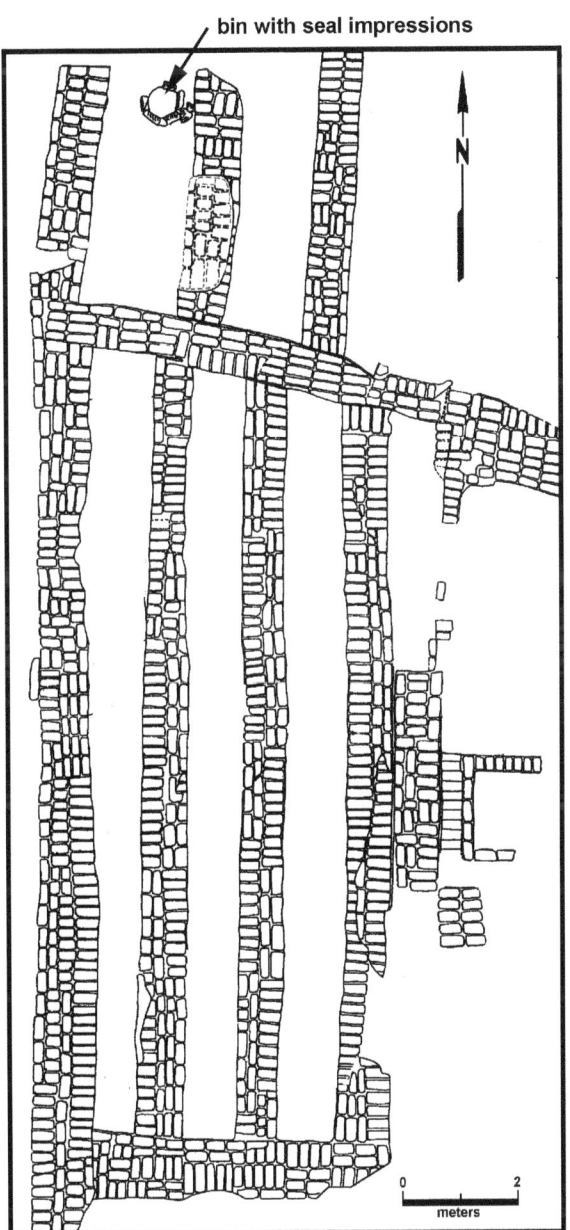

Figure 7.1. Plan of building with parallel walls and location of sealing bin (from Shinde et al., 2003)

to support the walls of the bin or as steps up to the opening (Figure 7.2). Of the 249 sealings found at Gilund, 214 were found in this bin. Eight more were found in a large, carefully lined pit located in trench 11, just to the east of the parallel wall structure.

The impressions of least ten different seals have been identified on the sealings. All of the designs are

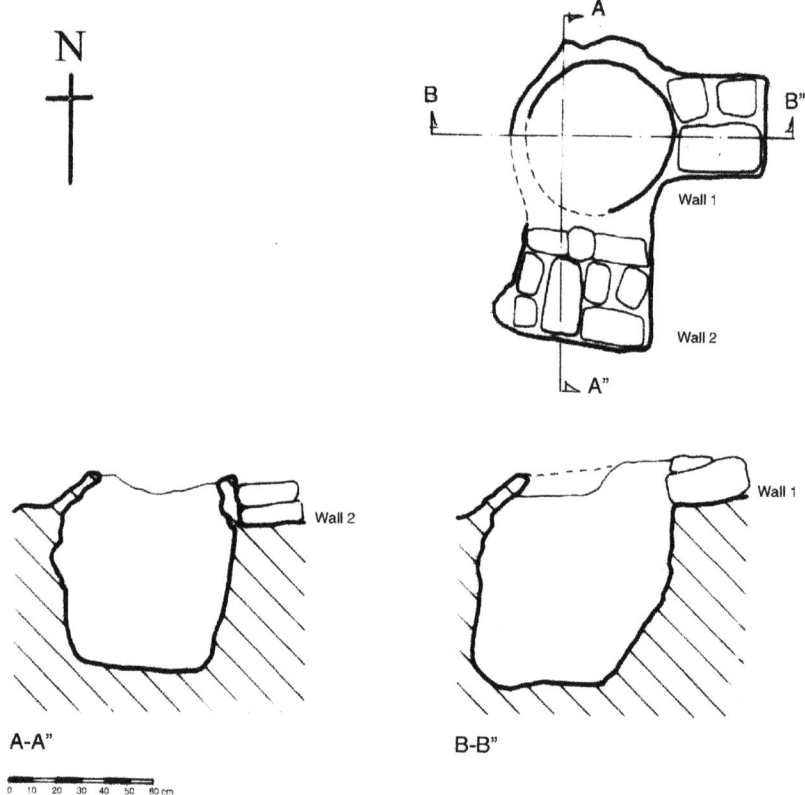

Figure 7.2. Sealing bin, plan and profile

geometric, and often consist of repeated motifs. Eight of these designs can be reconstructed with reasonable certainty and are shown in Figure 7.3. These include a round seal with five concentric circles around a central circular element with two lines going through it (Figure 7.3, no.1); two square seals with four-petalled flowers, one with a diamond shaped centre (Figure 7.3, no. 2) and one with a bull's-eye in the middle (Figure 7.3, no. 3); a rectangular cross-hatched seal with a solid rectangular frame (Figure 7.3, no. 4); a seal of unknown shape with two circular elements, one a series of concentric circles and the other a variation on a sunburst (Figure 7.3, no. 5); a circular sunburst seal (Figure 7.3, no. 6); and a square seal with four bull's-eyes at the corners and a round central element (Figure 7.3, no. 8). The last reconstructed seal (Figure 7.3, no. 7) is perhaps the most complex. It consists of a teardrop shape with a round 'eye'. Four curved parallel lines that seem to be continuations of the circular 'eye' articulate the interior of the teardrop shaped body. The lower line of the teardrop joins two other lines to form the outermost of three nested triangles that form the left side of the seal. Furthest to the left are four deeply impressed half-ovals which seem to form a sort of tail. Seals 1, 2, 3, 5 and 6 made the large majority of the impressions found on the sealings found in the bin at Gilund (see Figure 7.4), and all seem to have been used multiple times. Seals 4, 7 and 8, on the other hand, have been identified on only one sealing each. Most of the remaining designs found on the sealings were too fragmentary to be reconstructed but seem to include double and quadruple spirals, more concentric circles and possibly a second 'fish' seal.

In addition to the seal impressions, excavators also found a group of terracotta amulets that may have functioned as seals.[1] Most of these were found in the upper levels of the mound and can be divided into two groups. The 12 seal-amulets in the first group (Figure 7.5) are flat and usually pierced. Aside from S1.113, which is cruciform, and S2.061, which is decorated on both sides, they are all round or square in shape and have a design on one side and a flat back. The designs range from a simple square with four round holes as seen on S3.025 to more intricate designs with swooping lines forming a tulip or bucrania shape as seen in S1.114 and S2.061, or a complex concentric circle design like that seen in S5.216. The most impressive of the flat amulets found at Gilund is S1.113, an amulet in the shape of a stepped cross with a round piercing within a square frame. It is this motif that is strongly associated with the cultures of Central Asia at the turn of the second millennium BC.

---

[1] I have referred to these objects as seal-amulets because this is term most commonly used term for materials of this type, although there is, in fact, little evidence that they were ever used for sealing. While it has been suggested that the lack of a handle or knob would have made it difficult to use these seal-amulets for sealing, it should be pointed out that seals from Shahr-i Sokhta, which are also flat, were definitely used for sealing, as documented by the fact that impressions were found of some of the very seals that were found at the site (for example Tosi 1968: figs. 96 a, b)

Figure 7.3. Seals reconstructed from seal impressions (drawings by J. Jarrett)

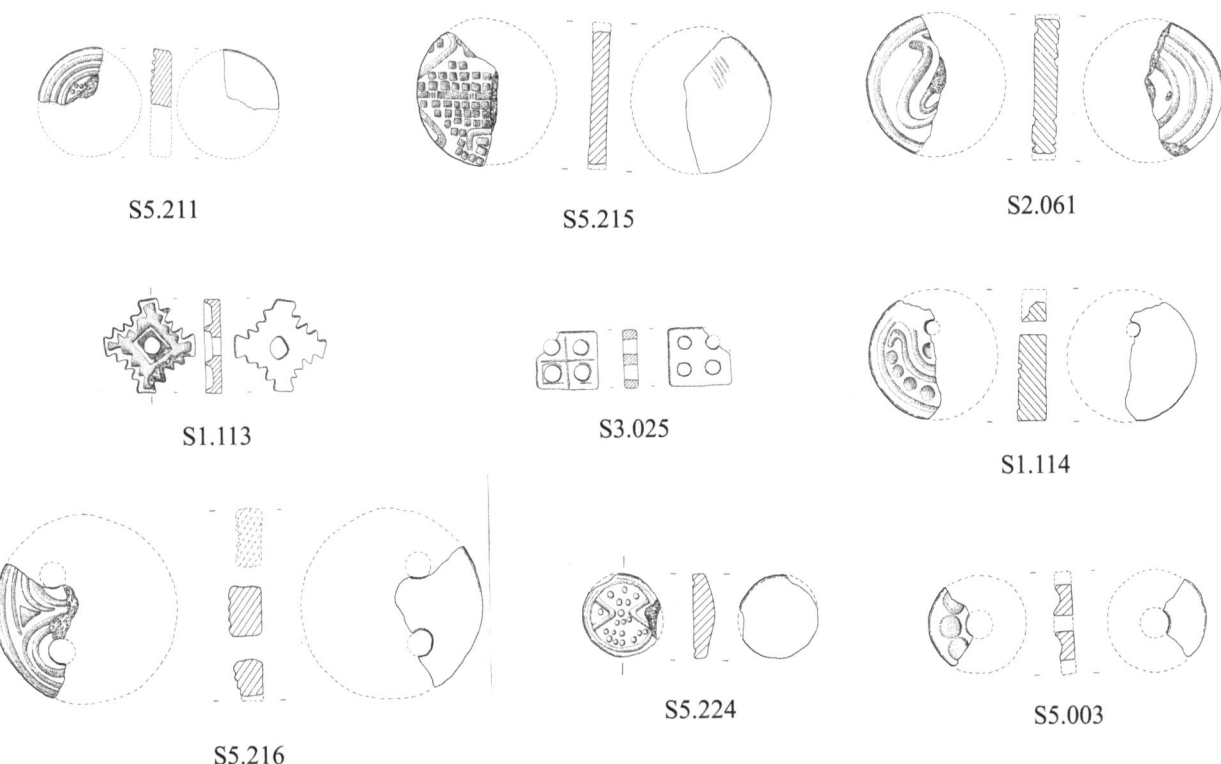

Figure 7.4. Seal-amulets (drawings by J. Jarrett)

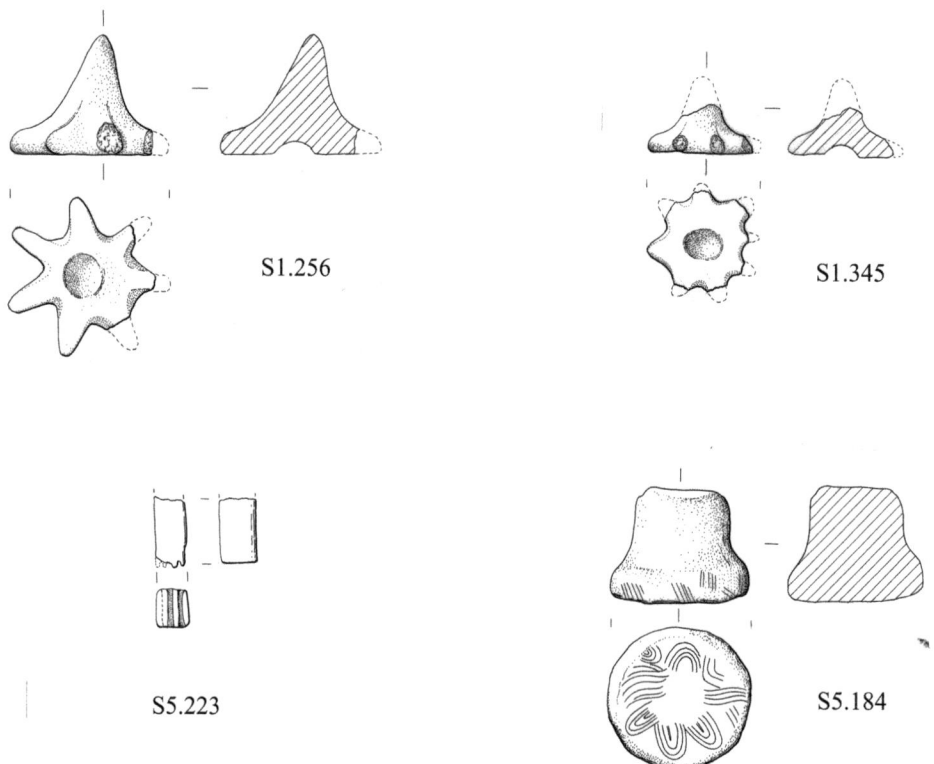

Figure 5. Stamps (drawings by J. Jarrett)

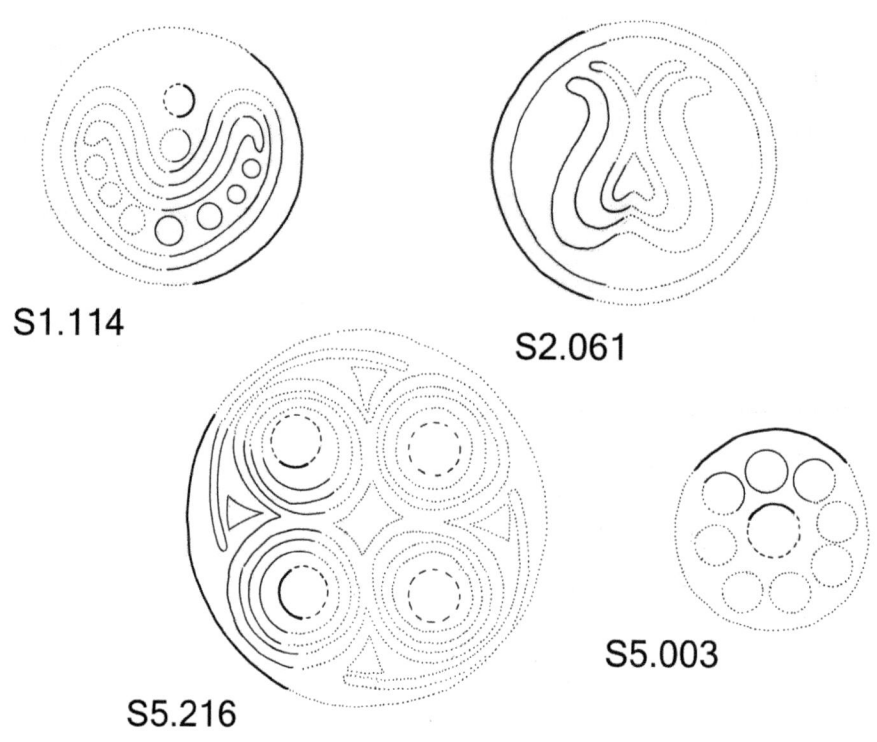

Figure 7.6. Reconstructed seal amulets (drawings by J. Jarrett)

S.5.216 with impression and sealing with concentric seal impression (GS 4.081)

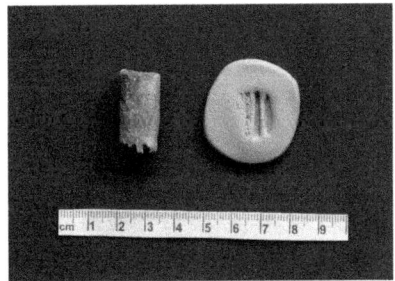

S5.223 and impression

sealing GS 5.004

Figure 7.7. Seal-amulets and sealings with comparable impressions

The second group (Figure 7.6) contains just four seals. These seals can be referred to as stamps based on their three-dimensional shapes and the presence of a projection that may have functioned as a handle on their backs. They vary in shape and decoration, but two, S1.256 and S1.345, are variations of the same many-pointed star motif, while a third, S5.184, is an unbaked mushroom-shaped stamp with an incised representation of a many pointed star. The fact that this object was unbaked suggests that it was probably never used as a stamp, but its shape and decoration leaves open for discussion the possibility that this may have been its intended purpose. The last stamp seal, S5.223, is a small squared-off rod with four parallel lines, one of which has broken off at one end.

The question of whether these seal-amulets and stamps were ever used for sealing remains open for debate. While none of the seal impressions found at Gilund appear to have been made by the seal amulets found at the site, the similarities between the impressions made by at least two of the amulets and the designs on some of the sealings cannot be ignored. The most interesting of these is the resemblance between the impression made by S5.216 and the concentric circle impression found on a large number of the sealings from Gilund (Figure 7.3, no. 1, Figure 7.8). While the seal is clearly not the same as the one that made these impressions, the similarity in the motifs suggests that it is simply a different rendering of the same motif, much in the same vein as the two different flower seals noted on the sealings (Figure 7.3, nos. 2-3). The parallel lines impressed on GS 5.004 also look as if they could have been made by a seal similar to S5.223 (Figure 7.8).

The seal-amulets from Gilund are unusual in that they are made of terracotta rather than stone or metal, the materials generally used to make compartmented stamp seals. Stamp seals made of terracotta were also found at Ahar (Deo 1969), Chanhu-daro (Mackay 1943, pls XLIX, L), Pirak (Jarrige and Santoni 1979, pls XLIV, XLV, figures 96-8), Tepe Hissar (Schmidt and Kimball 1937, H 1728, H 1785, H 2954, H 2582) and Konar Sandal (Madjidzadeh and Pittman 2008: Figure 28f), but they are the exception rather than the rule. In addition, only at Gilund, Ahar and Konar Sandal (and possibly two examples from Tepe Hissar, Schmidt and Kimball 1937, nos. H 1728, H 1785) do we find terracotta stamp seals that were designed to imitate compartment stamp seals made of copper or bronze.[2] It is also significant that the terracotta seals from Ahar and Gilund imitate compartment seals with closed backs, which Sandro Salvatori believes are the first to be produced (Salvatori 2000, 106ff). The seal-amulets from Ahar are the ones that most resemble those from Gilund, and certainly belong to the same cultural and stylistic milieu. Plasticine impressions taken of the terracotta seal-amulets show that their impressions would probably have been fairly rough, but legible. It does seem however that the impressions on many of the sealings were made by finer seals, possibly ones made of stone. The thickness of the lines of the impressions found on the Gilund sealings makes it unlikely that these impressions were made by metal seals, which would have produced much finer lines.[3]

---

[2] This imitation is particularly evident in the seal-amulet in the shape of a stepped cross from Gilund (S1.113) and in the seal amulet with scalloped edges from Ahar (Deo 1969, Figure 114, no.1).

[3] A good contrast of the impression made by a metal stamp seal as opposed to that made by a stone one can be seen in Asko Parpola's examination of 'bicultural' sealings found at Mohenjo-daro (Parpola 1994, 2006).

	Concentric Circle	Flower	Cross-Hatch	Spiral and ladder	Spiral	Sunburst	"fish"	Other	Sum
Shoulder of vessel	7	5		3		3		14	32
Rim of Vessel	7	9	1	4	1	3	2	24	50
Neck of vessel	5	6		4				10	25
Flat	3	9		2	4	1		10	29
Rope impression	2	4		1	1			7	15
Textile impression	1					1		2	4
Vessel decoration	3	3		1				4	11
Total number of impressions	28	14 with diamond centre 4 with round centre 44 total	1	14	5	7	3		

Figure 7.8. Seal frequency and readable impressions on backs of sealings

The most common motif found at Gilund is that of a four-petalled flower or rosette (Figure 7.3, nos. 2, 3), which is found on at least 20% of the sealings. The flower impressions were made by at least two different seals, both of which can be reconstructed as square with four tear-shaped petals that emanate from a central element. This element was square in one case and in the shape of a bull's eye in the second. The seal with the round centre was deeply carved with bold forms that emphasise the spaces between the petals as well as the petals themselves, while the one with the diamond centre was slightly smaller and appears to have been more delicately carved. The four-petalled rosette is a motif that is well known from sites in Iran, particularly Shahr-i-Sokhta and Shahdad. The examples from Shahr-i Sokhta (Baghestani 1997, no. 94; Salvatori 2000, Figure 11.9) are both copper/bronze compartmented stamp seals with closed backs and date to periods III and II.6 respectively. The flower is not placed within a square frame, but the shape of the petals is very similar to that seen on the impressions from Gilund. At Shahdad, four-petalled rosettes in square frames are found both on metal stamp seals (Hakemi 1997, 377, pl. 1a, nos. 2, 10) and on stamped impressions on pottery vessels (Hakemi 1997, 672, nos. 8, 33, 673, no. 41). A glazed steatite seal found at Harappa (Kenoyer 2001, Figure 3, no. 5) also has a similar motif of a four-petalled rosette in a square frame. The back of this seal is also decorated with at least five small concentric circles. The same motif is also found on slightly later seals from both Margiana and the Indus Valley. These include an early second millennium Murghab style stamp seal from Togolok 1 (Sarianidi 1998, no. 1350) and a round terracotta stamp seal from the post-Harappan Jukhar levels at Chanhu-daro (Mackay 1943, pl. L no. 7). Both of these seals are double sided, although the example from Togolok is square and made of chlorite and has an image of a griffin rather than a geometric motif on the other side.[4] Many more seals of this type were purchased in the market in Kabul (for example Sarianidi 1998, nos. 632-38, 744) and are thought to come from BMAC sites or cemeteries, but this paper focuses on the excavated material in the hopes of creating a better chronological framework for the material from Gilund.

Outside of the Ahar-Banas complex, the best excavated parallels for the concentric circle seal (Figure 7.3, no. 1), which is impressed on at least 28 of the 249 sealings excavated at Gilund, come from Altyn Tepe in Turkmenistan and from Shahr-i Sokhta and Shahdad in southern Iran. The example from Altyn is a round bronze stamp seal with a solid back (Masson and Kiiatkina 1981, 111, Figure 2, middle of the bottom row) that was found in the Tower mound. While no context is given for this seal, it is likely that it, like the other bronze compartmented seals from the site, can be dated to the final Namazga V levels of the city. The seal is broken, but preserves three small sets of concentric circles around a central rectangular element.[5] There are also two small semi-circles preserved in the areas between the larger circles along the outside of the seal. The seal from Shahr-i Sokhta, a surface find, is steatite and has a central element made up of a cross within a square and surrounded by at least four (originally probably six) sets of small concentric circles (Tosi 1968, Figure 100). The fragment that is preserved appears to be square or rectangular, but as it is broken on all sides it is possible that it was originally round. At Shahdad there are at least

---

[4] One double sided seal from Chanhu-daro (Mackay 1943: pl. L, no. 15) has an image of what may be a bird, but it is the only Jukhar stamp seal from the site with a non-geometric motif.

[5] Masson 1988 and Baghestani 1997 both have a drawing of a similar seal which is represented as complete and with a circular element in the centre, but Baghestani states that the illustration is wrong and that the seal has a rectangle in the centre, which suggests that this is in fact the same seal reproduced in Masson and Kiiatkina 1981.

two impressions of seals composed of multiple (usually four) small concentric circles found on pottery (Hakemi 1997, 674, nos. 77, 86). Other similar seals include a small square stamp seal made of glazed steatite with five concentric circles and central four-pointed star found in Kot Diji levels at Harappa (Kenoyer 2001, Figure 3, no. 7), and a broken round stamp seal with remnants of two concentric circles and part of a third from the early second millennium settlement on the island of Failaka in the Persian Gulf (Kjaerum 1983, no. 36). A faience stamp seal from the Jukhar levels of Chanhu-daro (Mackay 1943, pl. XLIX no. 2) has four sets of concentric semi-circles and a central element that resembles the one in the centre of the concentric circle seal from Gilund. On the other hand, a bronze stamp from the Middle Bronze Age levels of Gonur Tepe (Salvatori 2000, Figure 2) has six circles around a central circular element, but this seal may have more in common with six-petalled rosette seals seen elsewhere than with the concentric circle seals. While the Failaka and Chanhu-daro seals can be dated to the beginning of the second millennium BC, all the other examples seem to date to the second half of the third millennium.

The 'spiral and ladder' seal (Figure 7.3, no. 5) does not have any direct parallels in the corpus of seals excavated in Iran or Central Asia, but the two elements that make up the design, the large concentric circle and the variation on the sunburst, do find parallels throughout the area. Unfortunately, many of the best parallels for the sunburst, both as seen on the sunburst seal (Figure 7.3, no. 6) and on the 'spiral and ladder' seal, come from the antiquities market (for example Sarianidi 1998, nos. 780-7), but there are a few comparable examples from excavated contexts, particularly several seals found in the Jukhar levels of Chanhudaro, and in levels II and III at Tepe Hissar. The earliest of these are probably the two terracotta sunburst seals from Hissar (Schmidt and Kimball 1937, H1785, H1964), which both have a set of small concentric circles in the centre. A copper stamp seal with a long handle, also from Tepe Hissar, has a design that consists of a central circle with an illegible design in the centre, and a series of straight lines radiating out from it. A broken circular stamp seal with a round central element and arms radiating out to an outer double frame from the post-Akkadian (Piggott 1943) levels at Anau (Pumpelly 1908, 152, Figure 256, pl. 31, no. 16) probably also belongs to this group. The seals from Chanhu-daro (Mackay 1943, pl. XLIX, no. 5, pl. L, no. 13) are also terracotta and both have lines radiating out from a single central circular element. In addition to the seals, an impression of a stamp seal with a design of a 'circle surrounded by a notched border' from level IVC at Tepe Yahya (Pittman 2001, p. 240, no. 4, Figure 10.4) can also be compared to the sunburst imagery from Gilund. Large concentric circles are perhaps more common, and seals with this motif have been found everywhere from Tepe Hissar (Schmidt and Kimball 1937, H2954, H3776, H4645) and Anau (Pumpelly 1908, 169 Figure 401, pl. 45, no. 9) to Ahar (Deo 1969, 176 nos. 1, 3).

The stepped-cross motif found on the seal-amulet S1.113, which is so commonly associated with the BMAC, is also well documented throughout Central Asia, Iran and even as far as Mari in Syria (Beyer 1989) in the second half of the third millennium BC. Examples of stepped cross seals were excavated at Altyn Tepe and Mundigak in Central Asia, as well as at Shahdad and Shahr-i Sokhta in Iran. Stone seals in the shape of a stepped cross are found as early as period II at Shahr-i Sokhta (Ferioli et al., 1979, 8-9), and Namazga IV at Altyn Tepe (Masson 1988: pl. XVI, no. 11). Both Susanne Baghestani (1997) and Sandro Salvatori (2000) have studied this motif in detail and their work does not need to be reiterated here, except to point out that this motif does in fact have a very long life throughout Middle Asia and is not limited in its existence to the BMAC, although it does seem to experience a resurgence in this latter culture (as do copper compartmented seals in general). The best known example from the Indus Valley is a seal in the shape of a stepped-cross with an eagle inside that was found in the later levels of Harappa (Vats 1940, pl. XCI, no. 255). This seal conforms closely to the stepped cross seals associated with the BMAC, which often depict animals or fantastic creatures within a stepped cross or lozenge shaped seal.

The last comparison is not to a Gilund seal or impression, but rather to the fine circular seal with the scalloped edges found by Sankalia at Ahar (Deo 1969, 188 Figure 114 no. 1). This seal, which, like the stepped cross seal found at Gilund appears to have been made as an imitation of a metal or stone compartmented stamp seal, can be compared to examples excavated in Namazga V contexts at Altyn Tepe (Masson 1988, pl. XXXIX.7, pl. XXIX, 6) and found on the surface at Gonur Tepe (Salvatori 2000, Figure 9.5). The motif itself almost seems to be a variation between a simple cross with rounded edges and the pinwheel of birds' heads that becomes common at the beginning of the second millennium. A bronze seal found at Kelleli 1 (Masson 1988, 92, Figure 27) and dated to Namazga V shows a combination of the scalloped elements and the birds' heads.

In conclusion, while preliminary discussions of the Gilund sealings focused on the possible BMAC origins of the iconography on the seals and seal impressions from Gilund (Possehl et al., 2004; Shinde et al., 2005), a secondary analysis focusing only on provenanced comparanda shows that the imagery on these seals falls within a longstanding glyptic tradition that existed throughout Middle Asia from the beginning of the third millennium through the middle of the second millennium BC and that the best parallels for most of the motifs can in fact be dated to the second half of the third millennium. Geographically, the parallels come from sites as far away as Mari in Syria and as close as Ahar, a mere 80 kilometers away.

The broad distribution of BMAC artefacts at the end of the third/beginning of the second millennium BC is a well-known and extensively studied phenomenon (see

Geographic Zone	Site	Period	Dates
Syria	Mari	Akkadian	c. 2400-2200 BC
Turkmenistan	Namazga	I	c. 4800-4000 BC
		II	c. 4000-3500 BC
		III	c. 3500-3000 BC
		IV	c. 3000-2500 BC
		V	c. 2500-2100 BC
		VI	c. 2100-1700 BC
	Altyn Tepe	Excavation 1, levels 9-14	c. 3500-3000 BC
		Excavation 1, levels 4-8	c. 3000-2500 BC
Margiana	Gonur	Middle Bronze Age	c. 2500-2100 BC
		BMAC Phase	c. 2100-1500 BC
Bactria	Sapalli Tepe		c. 2000-1900 BC
	Dashly	1	c. 2100-1900 BC
		3	c. 1900-1700 BC
Khorasan	Tepe Hissar	I	c. 4300-3600 BC
		II	c. 3600-2600 BC
		III	c. 2600-2200 BC
Iran	Shahdad	Early graves	c. 2800-2200 BC
		Later graves	c. 2200-1700 BC
	Shahr-i Sokhta	I (levels 7-10)	c. 3100-2650 BC
		II (levels 5-6)	c. 2650-2450 BC
		III (levels 3-4)	c. 2450-2100 BC
		IV (levels 0-2)	c. 2100-1750 BC
Afghanistan	Mundigak	I	c. 4300-4000 BC
		II	c. 4000-3500 BC
		III (1-6)	c. 3500-2500 BC
		IV (1-3)	c. 2500-1900 BC
		V	c. 1900-
Baluchistan	Sibri	I-II	c. 2400-1750 BC
	Pirak	I (A,B)	c. 1900-1600 BC
		II (A,B)	c. 1600-1000 BC
Indus Valley	Harappa	1 (Ravi Phase)	c. 3300-2800 BC
		2 (Kot Diji Phase)	c. 2800-2600 BC
		3A (Harappa A)	c. 2600-2450 BC
		3B (Harappa B)	c. 2450-2200 BC
		3C (Harappa C)	c. 2200-1900 BC
		4 (Harappa/late Harappa Transitional	c. 1900-1800? BC
		5 (Late Harappa)	c. 1800?-1300 BC
	Chanhu-daro	Harappan	c. 2500-1900
		Jhukar	c. 1900-1500?
Rajasthan	Gilund	Early Ahar-Banas	c. 3000-2500 BC
		Middle Ahar-Banas	c. 2500-2000 BC
		Late Ahar-Banas	c. 2000-1700 BC

Figure 7.9. Chronological Chart[6]

[6] Dates adapted from (Baghestani 1997; Possehl and Rissman 1992; Kenoyer 1998; Shaffer 1992; Kohl 1992)

Figure 7.9). However, less is known about the networks that existed throughout Middle Asia in the second half of the third millennium. The discovery of common Iranian motifs this far east is unexpected and seems to call for a re-examination of past interpretations of the contacts between cultures in Southern and Central Asia during this period. The discovery of this material at Gilund suggests that these networks, in fact, spread much farther than previously believed. The increasing evidence for contact and influence within this Middle Asian Interaction Sphere makes it possible to closely examine the material and to attempt to identify the patterns of this contact.

Bibliography

Baghestani, S. 1997. *Metallene Compartimentsiegel aus Ost-Iran, Zentralasien und Nord-China, Archèaologie in Iran und Turan, Bd. 1.* Rahden/Westphalia, Verlag, Marie Leidorf.

Beyer, D. 1989. Un nouveau témoin des relations entre Mari et le monde Iranien au IIIéme millénaire. *Iranica Antiqua* XXIV, 109-120.

Deo, S. B. 1969. Terracotta objects. In H. D. Sankalia, S. B. Deo and Z. D. Ansari (eds), *Excavations at Ahar (Tambavati)*, 176-98. Pune, Deccan College.

Ferioli, P., E. Fiandra and S. Tusa. 1979. Stamp seals and the functional analysis of their sealings at Shahr-i Sokhta II-III (2700-2200 B. C.). In J. E. Lohuizen-de Leeuw (ed.) *South Asian Archaeology 1975*, 7-26. Leiden, E. J. Brill.

Hakemi, A. 1997. *Shahdad: Archaeological Excavations of a Bronze Age Center in Iran*. Rome, IsMEO.

Hiebert, F. T. and C. C. Lamberg-Karlovsky. 1992. Central Asia and the Indo-Iranian borderlands. *Iran* 30, 1-15.

Jarrige, J. F. and M. Santoni. 1979. *Fouilles de Pirak*. Paris, Diffusion de Boccard.

Kenoyer, J. M. 1998. *Ancient Cities of the Indus Valley Civilization*. Oxford, American Institute of Pakistan Studies and Oxford University Press.

2001. Early developments of art, symbol and technology in the Indus Valley tradition. Available from http://www.harappa.com/indus3/e1.html.

Kjaerum, P. 1983. *Failaka/Dilmun: The Second Millennium Settlements. Vol. 1.1, The Stamp and Cylinder Seals: Plates and Catalogue Descriptions, Jysk Arkæologisk Selskabs skrifter, 17, 1*. Aarhus.

Kohl, P. L. 1992. Central Asia (Western Turkestan): Neolithic to the Early Iron Age. In R. W. Ehrich (ed.) *Chronologies in Old World Archaeology*, 179-95. Chicago, University of Chicago Press.

Mackay, E. J. H. 1943. *Chanhu-Daro Excavations, 1935-36*. New Haven, CT, American Oriental Society.

Madjidzadeh, Y., and H. Pittman. 2008. Excavations at Konar Sandal in the region of Jiroft in the Halil Basin: The first preliminary report, *Iran* 46, 69-104.

Masson, V. M. 1988. *Altyn-Depe*. University Museum Monograph 55. Philadelphia, University Museum Press.

Masson, V. M., and T. P. Kiiatkina. 1981. Man at the dawn of civilization. In P. L. Kohl (ed.), *The Bronze Age Civilization of Central Asia: Recent Soviet Discoveries*, 107-34. Armonk, New York, M. E. Sharpe.

Parpola, A. 1994. *Deciphering the Indus script*. New York, Cambridge University Press.

Parpola, A. 2006. Administrative contact and acculturation between Harappans and Bactrians: Evidence of sealings and seals. In C. Jarrige and V. Lefèvre (eds), *South Asian Archaeology 2001*, 267-74. Paris, Éditions Recherche sur les Civilisations.

Piggott, S. 1943. Dating the Hissar sequence–the Indian evidence. *Antiquity* 17, 169-182.

Pittman, H. 2001. The glyptic art of period IV. In D. T. Potts, C. C. Lamberg-Karlovsky, H. Pittman and P. L. Kohl (eds), *Excavations at Tepe Yahya, Iran, 1967-1975: The Third Millennium*, 231-68. Cambridge, Peabody Museum of Archaeology and Ethnology, Harvard University.

Possehl, G. L. and P. C. Rissman. 1992. The chronology of prehistoric India: From earliest times to the Iron Age. In R. W. Ehrich (ed.), *Chronologies in Old World Archaeology*, 465-90. Chicago, University of Chicago Press.

Possehl, G. L., V. Shinde and M. Ameri. 2004. The Ahar-Banas complex and the BMAC. *Man and environment* 29(2), 18-29.

Pumpelly, R. 1908. *Explorations in Turkestan: Expedition of 1904. Volume II: Prehistoric Civilizations of Anau: Origins, Growth, and Influence of Environment*. Washington, D. C., Carnegie Institution of Washington.

Salvatori, S. 2000. Bactria and Margiana seals: A new assessment of their chronological position and a typological survey. *East and West* 50 (1-4), 97-145.

Sarianidi, V. I. 1998. *Myths of ancient Bactria and Margiana on its Seals and Amulets*. Moscow, Pentagraphic.

Schmidt, E. F. and F. Kimball. 1937. *Excavations at Tepe Hissar, Damghan*. Philadelphia, University of Pennsylvania Press.

Shaffer, J. G. 1992. The Indus Valley, Baluchistan, and Helmand traditions: Neolithic through Bronze Age. In R. W. Ehrich (ed.), *Chronologies in Old World Archaeology*, 441-64. Chicago, University of Chicago Press.

Shinde, V., G. L. Possehl and M. Ameri. 2005. Excavations at Gilund 2001-2003: The seal impressions and other finds. In U. Franke-Vogt and H.-J. Weisshaar (eds), *South Asian Archaeology 2003*, 159-169. Aachen, Linden Soft.

Tosi, M. 1968. Excavations at Shahr-i Sokhta, a Chalcolithic settlement in the Iranian Sistan. Preliminary report on the first campaign, October-December 1967. *East and West* 18, 1-66.

Vats, M. S. 1940. *Excavations at Harappa: Being an Account of Archaeological Excavations at Harappa Carried out between the Years 1920-21 and 1933-34*. Delhi, Government of India.

8. Indices of Interaction: Comparisons between the Ahar-Banas and Ganeshwar Jodhpura Cultural Complex

Uzma Z. Rizvi

As part of a larger publication on Gilund excavations, this chapter refocuses attention on interactions marked in the materiality of cultures beyond the Ahar-Banas Complex, specifically, in comparison with that of the Ganeshwar Jodhpura Cultural Complex (GJCC). Towards that goal, this chapter will first contextualise the GJCC and provide background for the types of artefacts unique to the GJCC corpus. Due to the relatively early stages of research in the GJCC, this chapter will focus primarily on ceramic comparisons, although some copper arrowheads are also referred to in this study.

There are some very clear limits to this project; firstly, that the ceramic corpus of both complexes is understudied and thus any result presented here is used to further interpretation, not necessarily to determine final results. This work is based on stylistic evaluations used specifically to gauge which time period might provide the best contrast for understanding contact and interaction between the GJCC and the Ahar-Banas Complex. In the resulting assessment, I argue that given the few mid-third millennium BC overlaps in ceramic style, it may prove to be a more fruitful venture to study interaction in an earlier time period between the two complexes and earlier settlements at Bagor; and in tandem with that shift, to look at the connections between the production of microliths and copper arrowheads. Additional excavations and artefact studies are needed to develop this interpretation, but studies such as that presented here help with retooling research questions and are thus useful.

Contextualising the GJCC

Located in Northeastern Rajasthan, the GJCC is a collection of third millennium BC settlements bound together by a shared cultural language that encompass similarities in material culture, production of copper tools, and geographic proximity to copper mines (Agrawala and Kumar 1982; IAR 1972-73; 1973-74; 1979-80; 1981-82; 1983-84; 1987-88; 1988-89; Hooja and Kumar 1997; Rizvi 2007). The GJCC is east of the Harappan culture, to the north-east of Ahar-Banas Complex, north/north west to the Kayatha Culture and at a later date, west of the OCP-Copper Hoard sites (Figure 8.1). Located within the regions of the Aravalli Hill Range, primarily along the Kantli, Sabi, Sota, Dohan and Bondi rivers, the GJCC is the largest copper producing community in third millennium BC South Asia, with 385 sites documented (Rizvi 2007, 192-222). Archaeological indicators of the GJCC were documented primarily in Jaipur, Jhunjhunu, and Sikar districts of Rajasthan, India, and include Incised ware, Reserved Slip ware and copper artefacts (Figure 8.2). This part of India is known for its farming and pastoral resources, as well as for minerals, the most important of which is copper. Khetri, the largest copper source in Rajasthan, has been exploited since antiquity, and continues today as one of the major resources for copper production in India.[1]

GJCC is synonymous with the Ganeshwar Culture, Jodhpura Culture, Ganeshwar-Jodhpura Copper Complex and the Ganeshwar-Jodhpura Culture (Agrawala and Kumar 1982, 130; Agrawal et al. 1978; Dikshit and Sinha 1982, 120; Hooja and Kumar 1997, 323-324). This study will refer to this area as the Ganeshwar Jodhpura Cultural Complex (GJCC) based upon the initial reports by R. C. Agrawala and V. J. Kumar; a complex based on the two type sites, Ganeshwar (Tehsil Neem Ka Thana; District Sikar; geo coordinates N 27° 40' 46", 75° 48' 93" E) and Jodhpura (Tehsil Kot Putli; District Jaipur; geo coordinates: N 27° 35' 51", 76° 06' 85" E). Choosing to name the cultural area as a complex simultaneously honors the terminology that Agrawala and Kumar provided and does not limit the understanding of the area as connected to one site or function.

The GJCC 2003 survey results are available in my PhD dissertation (Rizvi 2007) and have been presented at previous EASAA meetings (London 2005) and thus are not extensively discussed in this chapter except to provide context to the comparison. The survey results include GJCC settlement sites, sites covered with vitrified metal waste, sites that had visible surface evidence for furnaces and smelters, sites where copper raw material may be mined or collected, and sites where copper hoards had been reported from local newspapers.

The material culture that is characteristic of the GJCC includes ceramics, copper, microliths, and small finds. The small finds from the GJCC sites include beads, grinding stones, terracotta cakes/lumps, and various bone/shell objects such as bangles and beads. Grinding stones, saddle querns, morters, and pestles are found at most GJCC sites (Rizvi 2007). A vast majority of the microliths at Ganeshwar demonstrate a well-articulated geometric industry (IAR 1981-82, 61-62). Raw material for the microliths includes quartz, chert, chalcedony and jasper (IAR 1981-82, 61-62; Rizvi 2007).

The ceramics from the GJCC are largely wheel-made, with few examples cited as hand made (IAR 1987-88, 101-102). The corpus is broadly divided into three

---

[1] For colonial accounts of copper exploitation in this region, see *Imperial Gazetteer of India: Rajputana 1908*, pp. 52, 71.

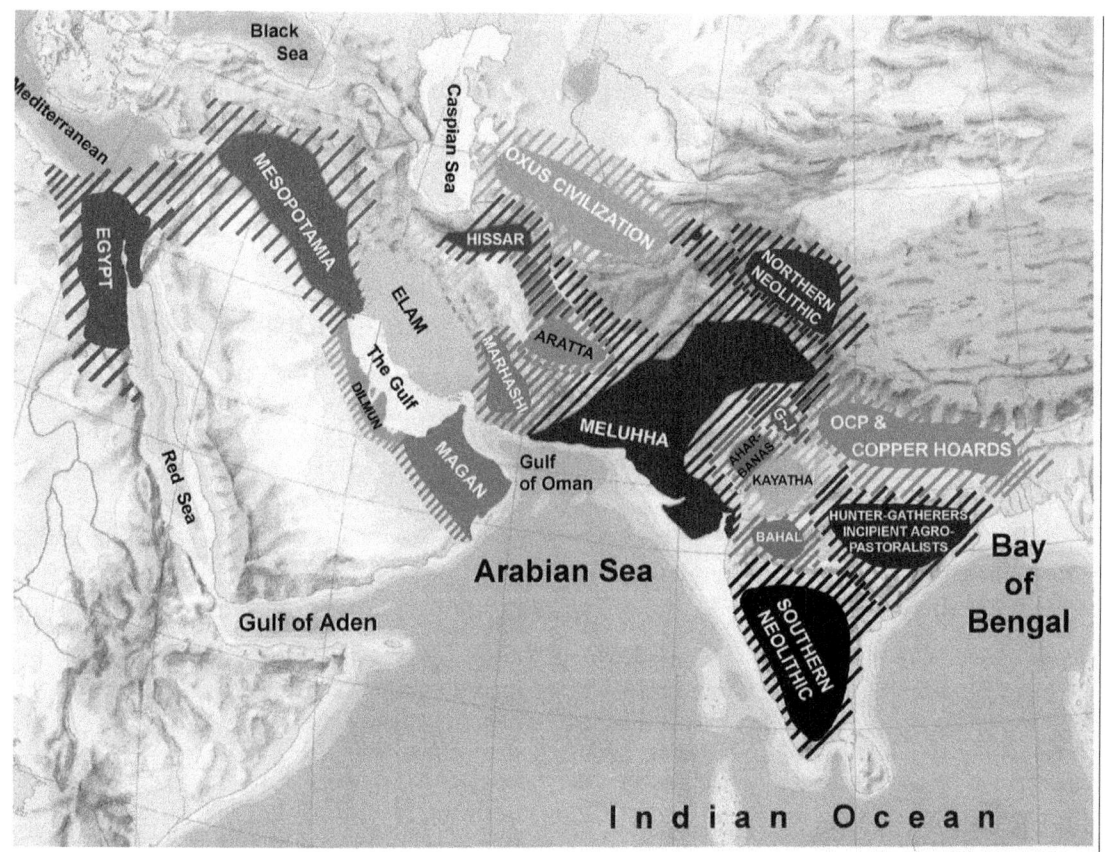

Figure 8.1 Map of Middle Asian Interaction Sphere (MAIS) (Map courtesy of G. L. Possehl)

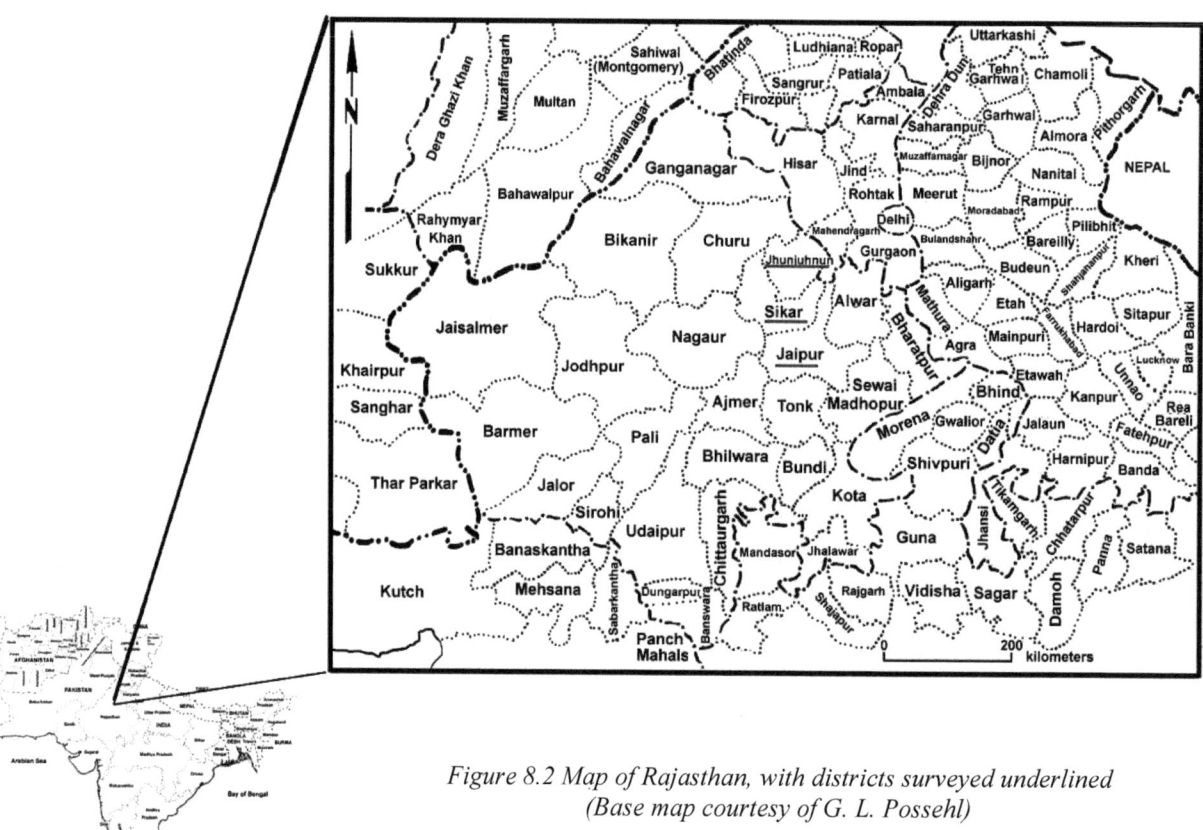

Figure 8.2 Map of Rajasthan, with districts surveyed underlined (Base map courtesy of G. L. Possehl)

Figure 8.3 GJCC ceramic assemblages Top Left: Ganeshwar surface survey 2000, medium red ware. Bottom Left: Reserved Slip Ware, Courtesy Hawa Mahal, Jaipur. Right: Incised Ware, Courtesy Hawa Mahal, Jaipur.

categories based on ware types, that is, coarse, medium and fine (Figure 8.3). The following descriptions are based on excavators' notes and reports from IAR 1987-88 and survey in 2000 and 2003.

The coarse wares from the GJCC make up a small percentage of the corpus; they are predominantly of micaceous coarse clay, inadequately fired, with a dark smoky core, and remnants of reddish brown slip and are fragile and crumble easily. Vessel forms include jars and basins. In contrast, the medium wares are well-fired and sturdy vessels, manufactured with finely levigated clay, including some sherds with mica added as a tempering agent, represented by forms including dish-on-stand, basins, troughs, lids, jars, vases and bowls decorated with incised designs. Typically, the vases have vertical handles attached between rim and shoulder. These red wares have painted decorations with brighter and evenly distributed colour, suggesting a faster and heavier wheel (IAR 1987-88, 101-102; Rizvi 2007).

The fine wares are wheel made and are lightweight, of finely levigated clay. There are three types of the fine red wares: dull red ware, fine red ware and Reserved Slip wares. Reserved Slip wares are distinct due to the specific

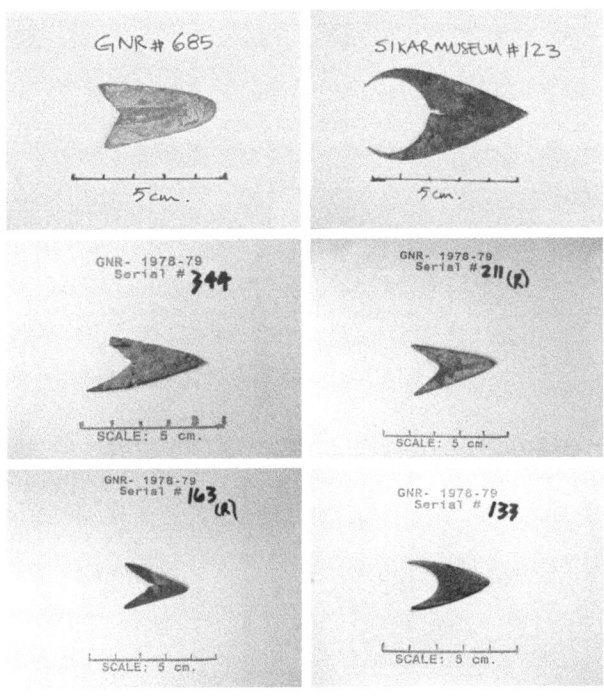

Figure 8.4 Copper arrowheads from Ganeshwar, 1978-79 excavations (Photographs taken by U. Rizvi)

decorative technique applied to the shoulder of the vessels. There are examples of this technique in various other forms from other sites in Rajasthan, such as at Early Harappan levels at Kalibangan, and Ahar-Banas sites, such as Balathal, and Ojiyana, however at the GJCC there are few examples of this technique in any other form beyond the vase/jar (Rizvi 2007).

Copper artefacts from the GJCC are a hallmark of the material associated with this culture, specifically, the forms of the copper arrowheads, celts, fishhooks and bangles. For example, the copper corpus from one season of excavation (1978-79) includes over 1000 pieces from Ganeshwar alone. Approximately 40% of the corpus consists of arrowheads, clearly marked as a special craft industry on site (Figure 8.4). Metallurgical analyses of two specimens from the site of Ganeshwar reveal objects that are manufactured with a high percentage of pure copper content, with traces of lead and arsenic alloying (Agrawala and Kumar 1982, 127-128 and see Figure 8.5).

Object	Cu	Sn	Fe	Pb	Zn	Ni	As	Ag
Celt	97.0	0.1	-	1.0	0.1	0.6	0.3	0.2
Arrowhead	96.5	0.2	0.2	0.03	0.25	0.04	1.0	0.3

Figure 8.5 Metallurgical analysis of copper materials from Ganeshwar, Rajasthan (Table taken from Agrawala and Kumar 1982, 127-128)

Dates (Cal.)	GJCC	Ahar-Banas	Harappan	Bagor (Site)	Kayatha (site)
3000 BC	Early	Early	Early	Period II	
2500 BC	Early	Early	Early	Period II	
2200 BC	Middle	Middle	Urban		Kayatha
2000 BC	Middle	Middle	Urban		Kayatha
1800 BC	Late	Late	Post Urban		Ahar-Banas

Figure 8.6: GJCC chronological framework in regional context

Dates (Cal.)	GJCC (Jodhpura)	Ahar-Banas	Harappan	Bagor	Kayatha	Noh
3000 BC	Incised ware, Reserved Slip ware, Copper Arrowheads and celts	Incised Ware, Reserved Slip Ware – Ahar Period IA	Copper Arrowheads from Kalibangan	Copper ArrowHeads From Burial Period II		
2500 BC	Incised ware, Reserved Slip ware, Copper Arrowheads and celts	Reserved Slip ware and incised ware – Balathal	Reserved slip ware from Kalibangan	Copper Arrowheads From burial Period II		
2200 BC	Copper arrowheads and celts	(Middle)	Copper Arrowheads from Banawali		Copper Celts (Kayatha)	
2000 BC	Copper Arrowheads and celts	(Middle)	Copper Arrowheads from Banawali		Copper Celts (Kayatha)	
1800 BC	(Late)	Incised ware - Ahar IB, GLD-2	(Post Urban)		(Ahar-Banas)	
1800-900	(GJCC/B&R)				(Malwa)	
800 BC	(PGW)					(PGW)

Figure 8.7 Chronological comparisons with examples used – GJCC in regional context

The GJCC illustrates an indigenous development that sustains a larger regional economic need for copper products. The underpinnings for such regional economic organisation were resource specialised complexes, which may have come together through certain variables, such as population increase, technological know-how or a simple adaptation to a landscape, but most significantly, these variables pivoted within highly circumscribed natural resource locales. As early as 2900 BC, the GJCC emerges as a community beginning to experiment with subsistence strategies, including fishing and hunting, evidenced by fishhooks and faunal remains, as well as some early farming as suggested by paleoclimate reconstructions, burnt anaj or seeds/grains in domestic structures, reconstructed irrigation pathways and grinding stones found in early contexts (IAR 1983-84, 71-72 and 95-96; Rizvi 2007). Active interactions with surrounding cultures are indicated through copper materials excavated in these disparate contexts (Agrawala 1987; Marshall 1931; Misra 1973; Sankalia et al. 1969). 2300 BC marks an increase in the production of copper based on the more complex organisation of the resource specialised community complexes within the GJCC. The maintenance of some form of cultural cohesion seems to stem from the creation of an economic niche based on copper. As the GJCC moves into later phases, there seems to be a diminishing of a distinctive cultural veneer, especially towards c. 1800 BC (Rizvi 2007) (See Figures 8.6 and 8.7).

The GJCC defines and is defined by its interactions, particularly its proximity to the Harappan Civilisation and the Ahar-Banas Complex. By occupying the space between two major cultural forces of the time, the GJCC emerges as a resource specialised community that has connections with both. In order to interpret such a cultural entity, it is crucial to have a better sense of how these groups interacted. The geographic location of the GJCC, in between the two large cultural centres of the Harappan and Ahar-Banas, precariously affects the interpretation of the region, requiring reconstructive configurations to account for and explore the ramifications of such a position. In order to explore such an argument, this chapter will now examine the potential material connections between the GJCC and the Ahar-Banas Complex, specifically ceramic stylistic links, keeping in mind chronological frameworks. The following section will provide some very basic contextual information about the Ahar-Banas Complex.

Brief Notes on the Ahar-Banas Complex

The Ahar-Banas culture is named after the type-site of Ahar, the River Ahar (a tributary of the Banas), and the proximity of the Banas River that flows through the region. There are over 100 sites listed as belonging to this complex, with only five excavated sites that have been instrumental in defining this cultural complex; the sites of Ahar (24° 35' N - 73° 43' E), Balathal (24° 43' N - 73° 59' E), Gilund (25° 01' N - 74° 15' E), Ojiyana (25° 53' N - 74° 21' E), and Purani Marmi (25° 08' N - 74° 27' E). These sites are located primarily in the Mewar region, along the banks of the Ahar, Banas, Berach, Gambhiri, Kothari and Khari Rivers, and their tributaries in the districts of Udaipur, Chittorgarh, Bhilwara, Dungarpur, Ajmer, Bundi and Tonk Districts; sites with Ahar Culture levels reported at sites in Madhya Pradesh at Jawad (24 36' N - 74 52' E), Kayatha, and Dangwada (Misra 1967, IAR 1982-83; Hooja 1988). The chronology of the Ahar-Banas Complex has been established through radiocarbon dates from Balathal and Gilund in which three phases are identified. Early Ahar-Banas 3000-2500 BC, Middle Ahar-Banas 2500-2000 BC, and Late Ahar-Banas 2000-1700 BC (Shinde et al. 2005, 158).

The site of Ahar was first excavated by A. K. Vyas of Rajasthan State Archaeology in 1950 and then re-excavated by R. C. Agrawal to shed more light on the chronology of the site (IAR 1954-55, 14-15; IAR 1955-56, 11). Agrawal divided the site into three major periods – Prehistoric, Early Historic, and Medieval. It was not until 1960-61 that Ahar was horizontally exposed through the collaborative work of Rajasthan State Archaeology and Deccan College (Pune) under the direction of H. D. Sankalia (IAR 1961-62, 42-50; Sankalia et al. 1969). These excavations revealed two cultural periods within the three phases. Period I, comprised of at least fifteen structural sub-phases, was argued to be chronologically linked to a copper using 'proto historic' period, with the earliest calibrated dates for Ahar Periods Ia, Ib and Ic being c. 2500 BC, c. 2100 BC and c. 1900 BC respectively (Ralph et al. 1973). Period II was marked by the use of iron, soak pits, and terracotta sealings with Brahmi characters. The associated Period IIa levels were marked with the use of Northern Black Polished Ware (NBP) and 3rd century BC material, and IIb, associated with Kushan period ceramics and Indo Greek coins. Period IIc was associated with late medieval (18th century AD) ceramics.

Evidence from the Ahar excavations indicates local agricultural practices, including the cultivation of rice and possibly millet (Sankalia et al. 1969; Vishnu-Mittre 1974). Artefactual evidence that aids in an agricultural reconstruction includes the documentation of saddle querns, grinding stones and mullers. Reconstructions of the ancient agricultural landscape were further developed through excavations at Balathal.

The site of Balathal, first reported in IAR in 1962-63, was recently (1993-1999) horizontally excavated by Deccan College (Pune) in collaboration with the Institute of Rajasthan Studies, Rajasthan Vidyapeeth, under the direction of V. N. Misra (IAR 1962-63, 18; Misra 1997; Misra et al. 1995 and 1997). The excavations expand the base for the reconstructions of agricultural landscapes in the Mewar region, specifically the early farming phases in this area. Radiocarbon dates from the excavations date the beginnings of the Ahar-Banas Complex to c. 3000 BC, making this complex contemporaneous to Early Harappan farming communities (Misra 1997; Shinde 2000).

The excavations at Balathal have provided new insights into the Ahar-Banas Complex, with beginnings as early as 3000 BC, architectural features suggesting the storage and the corralling of animals, as well as craft activities at the site. Additionally some sherds were found that indicate interaction with the Harappan Civilisation. Interconnections between sites of the Ahar-Banas Complex and other regional polities are important to note in order to contextualise the ancient landscape. The site of Gilund has demonstrated additional networks in the region, extending possibly to Central Asia.

The site of Gilund, in Rajsamand District, is by far one of the largest Ahar sites (about 17 hectares in site size), and was first reported as 'Bhagwanpura' by K. N. Puri in explorations conducted during 1957-58. B. B. Lal then excavated the site in 1959-60 (IAR 1959-60: 41-46). The site was initially chronologically categorised into three phases – the Ahar phase, Early Historic and Medieval (IAR 1959-60, 41-46). Calibrated radiocarbon dates of the site date it to 3000-1500 BC (Shinde *et al.* 2005). Excavations at the site of Gilund were co-directed by Gregory L. Possehl (University of Pennsylvania) and Vasant Shinde (Deccan College, Pune).

Excavations at Gilund have been set up to expand on the information from the Balathal excavations. The principle questions dealt with at Gilund include investigating the early village farming communities of Mewar, interregional interactions, socio-cultural aspects of the Ahar-Banas complex, local economic aspects of the Gilund site, and recontextualising the transition from Chalcolithic to Iron Age in Mewar (for more studies on Gilund, see other chapters and the forthcoming Gilund Excavation Report).

The excavations at Gilund have documented Ahar-Banas occupational levels, with five structural phases, the lower levels similar to material assemblages from Balathal, including evidence for Reserved Slip Ware. There is also some evidence of incised ceramics on the top of GLD-2 (V. Shinde and M. McCormick, pers. comm.). In terms of large-scale architecture, the excavations have documented a wall/circumvallation, parallel walls and large rectangular buildings. The area of the parallel walls is particularly interesting as this is the area where a bin with seal impressions was documented. The bin contained over 100 seal impressions made from both round and rectilinear seals (Shinde *et al.* 2005, 160). The design motifs have parallels with Chanhu Daro (Jhukar period), Pirak Periods I and II, Kot Diji, Nindowari, as well as parallels with examples of seals from the Bactria Margiana Cultural Complex (BMAC) (Shinde *et al.* 2005, 160-161). The sealings have been dated to the Middle Ahar-Banas period, suggesting very close connections and networks between the Ahar-Banas Complex and the Harappan Civilisation, as well as to sites in Central Asia (see Ameri this volume).

Excavations at the site of Ojiyana also provide some important evidence suggesting a closer connection between the Ahar-Banas and Harappan cultures. Ojiyana was first excavated in 1998 by the Jaipur circle of ASI under the direction of B. R. Meena, with additional excavations in 2000 under the joint directorship of B. R. Meena and A. Tripathi (Tripathi 2000).

Based on ceramic assemblages and associated finds, the site has been divided into four periods. Period I occupation comprises three phases of construction, beginning with thin mud brick floors as the only evidence, the second phase with stone foundations, and the third, wattle and daub residential structures of early farmers. Black and Red ware is the most distinctive pottery type of this time period, with additional red wares, grey wares, tan wares and black slipped wares also present. Also important to note is the documentation of a Harappan type faience bead and terracotta cakes, suggesting connections between the Mature Harappan cultures and this Ahar-Banas settlement (Tripathi 2001).

Comparison between Ahar-Banas Complex and GJCC

As demonstrated in the short section on the Ahar-Banas, many of the comparisons of the material culture have been usually directed towards the Harappan culture, not the GJCC. This section will provide a first look at how a systematic comparison between the GJCC and the Ahar-Banas might best be articulated.

K. N. Dikshit and A. N. Sinha point to resemblance in Ahar IA-IC red wares (Figure 8.8) to GJCC Red Slipped ware, citing a red ware industry at Ahar with incised decorations on the outer side (1982, 120-122). Further, they argue that typologically and stylistically, the ceramics are similar to those collected during their survey at Ganeshwar. If this comparison is correct, that would place GJCC within the range of Ahar Ia-Ic, that is, *c.* 2400-1400 cal. BC (Sankalia *et al.* 1969).

In comparing ceramics from the site of Balathal in his dissertation, Anupa Mishra has suggested little resemblance between the ceramics of the Ahar-Banas Culture and GJCC (2000). He argues that except for a similar incised decoration with the red wares of Phase Ia at Balathal (Figure 8.9), there is very little else which stylistically connects the two cultures.[2] He does however suggest that the only viable connections to be made could be illustrated through the occurrence of a similar type of Burnished Grey ware and a Reserved Slip ware at Ganeshwar.

The site of Gilund also has a few examples of incised wares from the top layers of GLD-2, in Trenches 50 and 56, as well as a Reserved Slip ware (Figure 8.10). Thus far, examples of the incised pieces from the Middle Ahar-Banas periods are not comparable to GJCC red wares, and although the Reserved Slip ware sherd is similar in technique and application, a single sherd example is difficult to justify in any argument.

---

[2] Mishra also mentions Phase Ib as heralded by the development of the Thick Red Slipped ware, with the rusticated body and incised designs. Thus, there is some question of why he chose to separate the types of incisions between Ia and Ib (2000, 328).

The incised designs from the GJCC that have been studied all demonstrate very simple designs, without any additional appliqué work, or complex arrangements of the incisions, in contrast to what the Ahar and Balathal materials indicate. Echoing Mishra's assessment, it would seem that there is not enough to go beyond the stylistic connections besides the fact that incisions exist on the corpus presented in this analysis. However, there are additional factors that can be taken into account, for example the types of vessels upon which the incisions are made.

It seems that early examples of globular pots from both Ahar and Balathal have examples of ridged shoulders and some with incised motifs on the body. Based on material collected in the surface survey in 2003, there are examples of parallel ridges on the shoulders, and based on the curvature of the body sherds with incised designs on them, it is most likely that they are part of the middle body section of globular pots. Additionally, from the site of Khatha Dhaba (GJC 117) (Figure 8.11), an example of a sherd with incisions shaped as triangular gauging marks was collected that is similar to the marks found on Balathal IIIb Thick Red Slip ware piece D112, Figure 127. This may suggest a later interaction between the two cultures, yet as a single example, it cannot hold much weight as an argument.

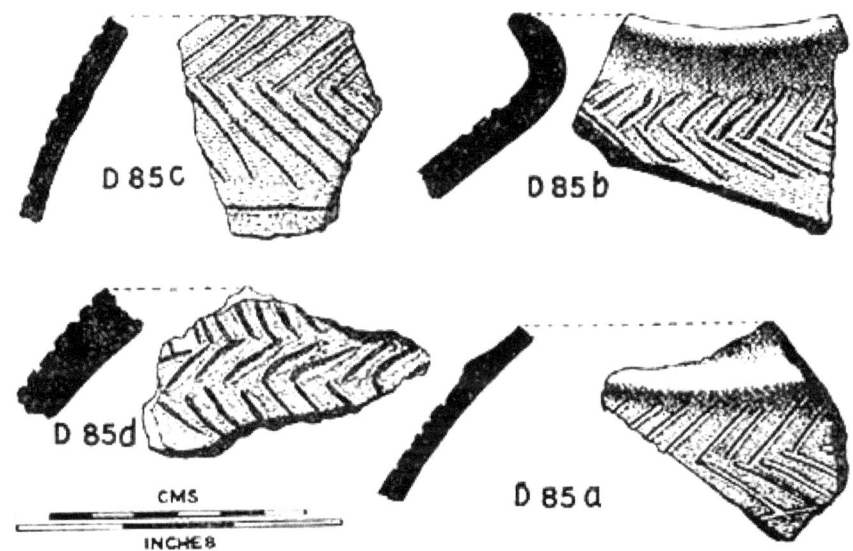

Figure 8.8 Incised ware from Ahar, Period IA (Sankalia, et al 1969: 77)

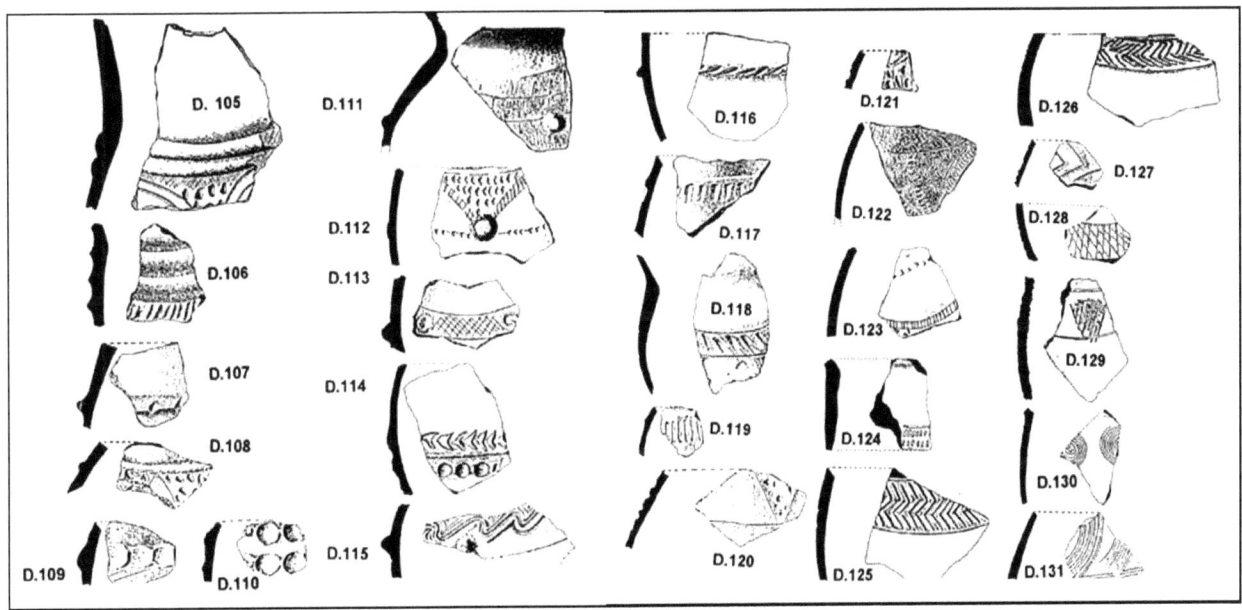

Figure 8.9 Incised ware from Balathal (Mishra 2000, figures 127 and 128)

Figure 8.10 Incised ware and Reserved Slip ware from Gilund (Courtesy of M. McCormick)

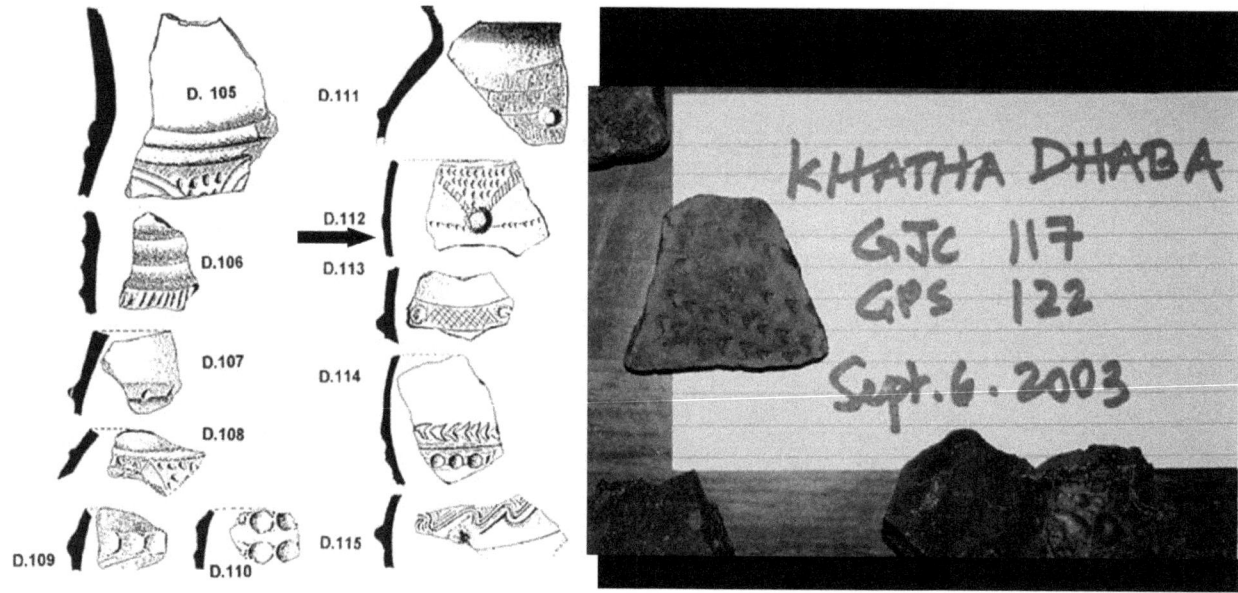

Figure 8.11 Comparison of Incised ware from Balathal (Mishra 2000) and from Khatha Dhaba (GJCC Survey 2003) (Misra 1970, 222)

The existence of Reserved Slip ware at all Ahar-Banas sites (Ahar, Balathal, Gilund, and Ojiyana) and in the GJCC, albeit in smaller percentages, is both the strongest and weakest argument for ceramic comparisons. These two specific types, that is, Incised ware and Reserved Slip ware are used for comparison because they are most easily identifiable, even though Incised ware (GJCC ware) and Reserved Slip ware were documented in small percentages at sites other than the main sites of Ganeshwar and Jodhpura. This may be because both main sites were excavated and thus these types of vessels were uncovered, while a surface survey is limited in its ability to represent material that may exist under the surface.

With such limited ceramic evidence, additional comparisons with other forms of material culture prove to be more useful, and this is one of the key areas where continued work is required, in particular on the copper material from the Ahar-Banas, such as the evidence of copper working at Gilund, and whether or not it represents primary or secondary manufacturing processes. There are roughly 40 copper pieces reported thus far from the Ahar-Banas Complex (Shinde, personal communication).

Early metallurgical studies conducted by Hegde from the site of Ahar, suggests that the copper used at the site originates from the Aravalli mines (1969, 226). This suggests a couple scenarios; firstly, Ahar had a direct source link to the Aravalli mines, and/or secondly, because GJCC was the source connection to the Aravalli mines, the two cultures were involved in processes of exchange and interaction. It is slightly unclear what sorts of networks might have been in place between the Ahar-Banas and the GJCC. This is due to the types (or lack) of archaeological information available for each of these cultural regions, in particular the GJCC. It is clear that Gilund exists at a higher level of socio-political complexity based on architecture, indications of large-scale trade (seals and sealings), and the extent of its interaction sphere, which, based on current information, has farther reaches than the GJCC. The archaeological indicators are suggestive of a relationship, through both general ceramic similarities, and the use of copper from the Aravalli mines, but are not conclusive. Whereas there are clear links established between the Ahar-Banas, Central Asia, and Iran, there is nothing of the sort with a culture just slightly to the North. Was the GJCC a hinterland for the Ahar-Banas – only to be used for resource exploitation?

Given the current lack of clear archaeological indicators to suggest that the Ahar-Banas was actively engaged in controlling copper as a resource from the GJCC, and with the vague material correlates, the actual connections between these two cultures is slight. In light of this statement, I suggest a shift of focus from the Middle GJCC (*c.* 2200-1800 BC) to the Early GJCC (*c.* 3000-2200 BC). Moreover, by investigating connections between Bagor, the Ahar-Banas Complex, and the GJCC, specifically looking at microlithic and copper intersections, there might be a firm foundation upon which to begin to answer some of these questions. New research from Gilund supports investigating this earlier time period, as early levels at Gilund have uncovered some incised ware that stylistically looks more akin to the GJCC Incised wares (Shinde, personal communication).

Bringing Bagor into the Mix

The site of Bagor (25° 21' N - 74° 23'E) is a small, 80 x 80 meters (0.64 hectares) site, excavated for one season by Deccan College (lead by V. N. Misra) and the University of Heidelberg, and then two later seasons by Deccan College (lead by V. S. Shinde), is located in the heart of the Mewar plain. The amended chronology for

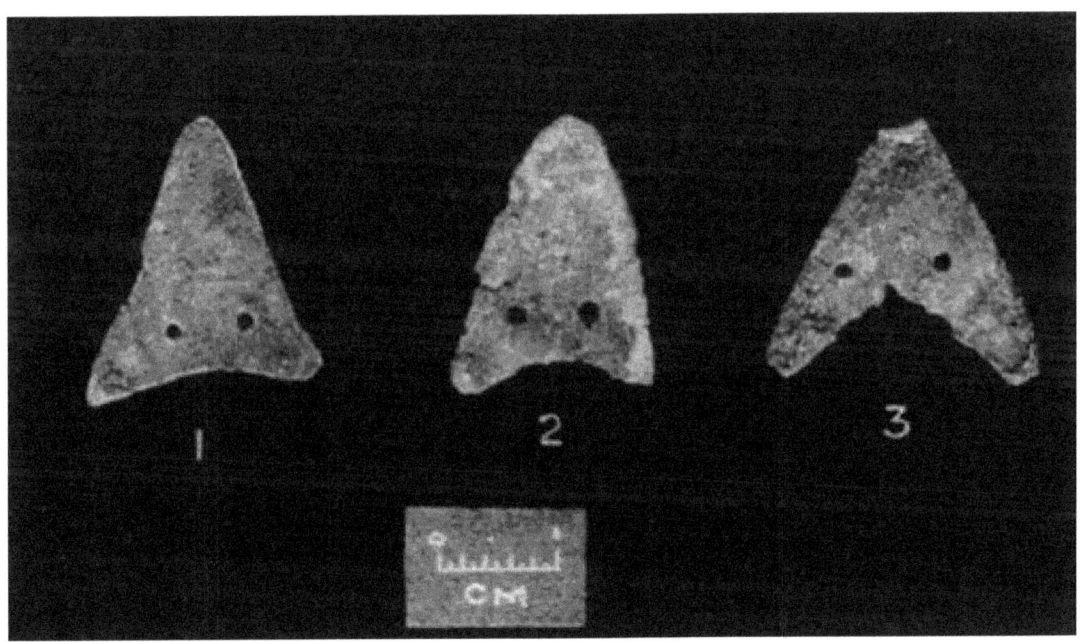

Figure 8.12 Arrowheads from Bagor burial, Phase II

Dates – BC	Ganeshwar	Bagor
> 2900	Period I (microlithic)	Period I (5500-2800) (microlithic)
2900-2500	Period II Phase I (Microliths, Incised Red Wares, Red Ware, some Cu artefacts)	Period II (Microlithic, and incised ware ceramics, burials with Cu arrowheads, and beads)
2500-2000	Period II Phase II (90% Cu Artefacts, Red Ware, Reserved Red Ware, Incised Red Ware)	Period II
2000-1800	Period II Phase II/Period III	Period II

Figure 8.13 Chronological comparison between Ganeshwar and Bagor

the site of Bagor has been presented by Possehl (1999, 481) as Phase I ca. 5500-2800 BC; Phase II ca. 2800-600 BC; and Phase III ca. 600 BC-200 AD (see also Misra 1973). It should be noted that there is evidence for microlithic sites elsewhere in Rajasthan as well, although no others have been so extensively excavated, except for some early work done at Tilwara (unpublished excavation). The microliths from Bagor form one of the largest corpus of lithic material from this time period in India. This industry was based on mass production of tools made from locally available quartz and chert as well as chert and chalcedony acquired from long-distances. Teresa Raczek's dissertation (2007 and see this volume) has investigated the lithic materials from Bagor and Gilund and presented a case for the two communities having shared skill sets in terms of lithic production – and important factor to keep in mind when developing a deeper understanding of the interactions in the region on the scale of daily practice.

A key phase to consider in this discussion is Phase II at Bagor. There are three burials associated with Phase II, all flexed, with the heads directed east, and associated with grave goods including pottery, ornaments, copper objects, and joints of meat (Misra 1973, 104). The use of copper in the burial was not accidental; the placement of the artefacts seems intentional. The copper arrowheads from the burial were compared by Misra to Mature Harappan arrowheads, in which there is a similarity in shape but the arrowheads are perforated (1970, 224). The copper arrowheads from Bagor do not find direct and easy comparisons in the GJCC corpus. Each Bagor arrowhead has two holes for tying the shaft, and a crude shape that does not compare to the complexity, and specificity of shapes of the GJCC arrowheads. However, the overall shape does indicate a rough imitation, rendition, or a precursor to the GJCC shapes. This is based on the rough shapes of the actual pieces that mimic overall shapes from GJCC, and the angle of the cut of arrowhead no. 3, which is visible by a simple visual comparison of Figures 8.4 and 8.12. It is also important to keep in mind the context of these artefacts, those from Bagor being in specifically burial context, and those from the GJCC being in settlement strata.

The ceramic comparison of Phase II potentially connects Bagor to the Ahar-Banas Complex, Kayatha, as well as the GJCC. Again, these ceramic comparisons are based on surface incisions that are problematic to determine unless handled in person. Based on the drawings and photographs of the material from the original excavations of Bagor Phase II (Misra 1973, 101, Figure 26, 1 and 10), there are similarities to Ahar Ia in the shape and form of incision (Sankalia et al. 1969, 77, Figure 36, D 83 C, D 85 C). Not surprisingly, there is also some resemblance of these incised wares with GJCC incised red wares. Dikshit and Sinha (1982) have discussed the similarities between the GJCC incised red wares and Ahar Ia-Ic. These stylistic ceramic comparisons align Bagor Phase II (2800-600 BC), Ahar Ia-Ic (2700-2500 BC), and Early GJCC (2900-2500 BC) to being coterminous. Even as these three ceramic comparisons line up neatly, it would be important to remember that the Bagor ceramic assemblage is handmade, and not wheel made, as are those from Ahar and Ganeshwar (Figure 8.13). In some sense, the mimicked form of the incised ceramic is similar to the rudimentary, possibly copied copper arrowheads in burial contexts.

The connections between these earlier phases, particularly in relation to the copper, microliths, and ceramics provide a more in depth context within which reevaluating the research question will result with clear material correlates indicating interaction. Such an understanding and investigation of interaction will also provide a more nuanced interpretation of the GJCC emergence within northeastern Rajasthan in the third millennium BC.

Acknowledgements

I would like to thank Drs Vasant Shinde and Teresa Raczek for inviting me to submit the presentation for publication. Special thanks also go to G. L. Possehl, R. C. Agrawala, V. J. Kumar, R. Hooja, J. Kharkwal, A. Mishra, M. McCormick, R. C. Swarnkar, L. Panwar, A. Mayaram, Archaeological Survey of India (Delhi and Jaipur), Department of Archaeology and Museums, State Dept of Rajasthan, University of Rajasthan, Jaipur, and the American Institute of Indian Studies. Survey 2003 Team: H. C. Misra, R. Sharma, J. Tennyson, N. Misra, A. Dhaka, F. Z. Rizvi, A. Nagar, S. Rizvi, and S. Singh. A Mellon Foundation Fellowship (2007) provided funding for this study; the GJCC Surveys, and subsequent write up was supported by the Zwicker Fellowship, University of Pennsylvania, George F. Dales Fellowship, Fulbright Hayes DDRA, Summer Field Funds, Department of Anthropology, University of Pennsylvania. Special thanks to Asad Pervaiz for image assistance.

Bibliography

Agrawal, D. P., R. Dhir, R. V. Krishnamurthy, V. N. Misra, S. Nanda and S. Rajguru. 1978. Multiple evidence for climatic change in Rajasthan. In H. S. Mann (ed.), *Arid Zone Research and Development*, 1-18. Jodhpur, Scientific Publishers.

Agrawala, R. C. 1987. Celts from Hansi, Haryana. In M. S. Nagaraja Rao (ed.), *Kusumanjali: New Interpretation of Indian Art and Culture*, C. Sivaramamurti Commemoration Volume, 115-16. Delhi, Agam Kala Prakashan.

Agrawala, R. C. and V. Kumar [1982] 1993. Ganeshwar-Jodhpura culture: New traits in Indian archaeology. In G. L. Possehl (ed.), *Harappan Civilization: A Recent Perspective*, 125-34. New Delhi, American Institute of Indian Studies and Oxford Publishing Co.

Archaeological Survey of India
1954-55. *Indian Archaeology: A Review* (IAR), 14-15.
1955-56. *Indian Archaeology: A Review* (IAR), 11.
1959-60. *Indian Archaeology: A Review* (IAR), 41-6.
1961-62. *Indian Archaeology: A Review* (IAR), 42-50.
1962-63. *Indian Archaeology: A Review* (IAR), 18.

1972-73. Excavation at Jodhpura, District Jaipur, *Indian Archaeology: A Review* (IAR), 29-30.

1973-74. Exploration in Districts Jaipur and Sikar, *Indian Archaeology: A Review* (IAR), 23-4.

1979-80. Explorations in Districts Alwar, Banswara, Bharatpur, Bhilwara, Chittaurgarh, Durgapur, Jaipur, Jhunjhunu, Sawai Madhopur, Sikar and Udaipur, *Indian Archaeology: A Review* (IAR), 62-5.

1981-82. Excavations at Ganeshwar, *Indian Archaeology: A Review* (IAR), 61-2.

1982-83. *Indian Archaeology: A Review* (IAR).

1983-84. Excavations at Ganeshwar, *Indian Archaeology: A Review* (IAR), 71-2

1987-88. Excavations at Ganeshwar, *Indian Archaeology: A Review* (IAR), 101-2.

1988-89. Excavations at Ganeshwar, *Indian Archaeology: A Review* (IAR), 76-8.

Dikshit, K. N. and A. K. Sinha. 1982. The Ganeshwar culture – an appraisal, *Puratattva* 11, 120-122.

Hegde, K. T. M. 1969. Technical studies in copper artifacts from Ahar. In H. D. Sankalia, S. B. Deo and Z. Ansari (eds), *Excavations at Ahar (Tambavati)*, 225-28. Deccan College Post-Graduate and Research Institute, Poona.

Hooja, R. 1988. *The Ahar Culture and Beyond: Settlements and Frontiers of 'Mesolithic' and Early Agricultural Sites in Southeastern Rajasthan, c. 3rd – 2nd Millennia BC.* British Archaeological Reports International Series 412. Oxford, British Archaeological Reports

Hooja, R. 1994. Ganeshwar and the 'Frontier Theory': A possible framework for understanding Ganeshwar – Harappan interaction, *Shodhak: A Journal of Historical Research* 23(69), 127-36.

Hooja, R. and V. Kumar. 1997. Aspects of the Early Copper Age in Rajasthan. In R. Allchin and B. Allchin (eds), *South Asian Archaeology 1995 Proceedings of the 13th Conference of the European Association of South Asian Archaeologists: Vol. 1*, 323-40. New Delhi, Oxford & IBH Publishing Co..

India, Government of. 1908. *Imperial Gazetteer of India: Provincial Series, Rajputana.* Calcutta, Superintendent of Government Printing.

Marshall, J. (Sir). 1931. *Mohenjo-Daro and the Indus Civilization.* 3 Vols. London, Arthur Probsthain.

Mishra, A. R. 2000. *Chalcolithic Ceramics of Balathal, District Udaipur, Rajasthan.* Unpublished Ph.D. Dissertation, Deccan College Post-Graduate and Research Institute.

Misra, V. N. 1967. *Pre-and Proto-History of the Berach Basin South Rajasthan.* Pune, Deccan College Postgraduate and Research Institute.

Misra, V. N. 1970. Cultural significance of three copper arrow-heads from Rajasthan, India, *Journal of Near Eastern Studies* 29 (4), 221-31.

Misra, V. N. 1973. Bagor: a late Mesolithic settlement in North West India. *World Archaeology* 5(1), 92-100.

Misra, V. N. 1997. Balathal: a Chalcolithic settlement in Mewar, Rajasthan, India: Results of the first three season's excavation, *South Asian Studies* 13, 251-73.

Misra, V. N., V. Shinde, R. K. Mohanty, K. Dalal, A. Mishra, L. Pandey and J. Kharakwal. 1995. The excavations at Balathal: Their contribution to the Chalcolithic and Iron Age cultures of Mewar, *Man and Environment* 20(1), 57-80.

Misra, V. N., V. Shinde, R. K. Mohanty, L. Pandey and J. Kharakwal. 1997. Excavations at Balathal, Udaipur District, Rajasthan (1995-1997), with special reference to Chalcolithic architecture, *Man and Environment* 22 (2), 35-60.

Possehl, G. L. 1999. *Indus Age: The Beginnings.* Philadelphia, University of Pennsylvania Press.

Raczek, T. 2007. *Shared Histories: Technology and Community at Gilund and Bagor, Rajasthan, India (c. 3000-1700 BC).* Unpublished Ph.D. Dissertation. University of Pennsylvania.

Ralph, E. K., H. N. Michael and H. Mark. 1973. Radiocarbon dates and reality, *MASCA Newsletter*, 9(1), 1-20.

Rizvi, U. 2007. *Configuring the Space Between: Redefining the Ganeshwar-Jodhpura Cultural Complex (GJCC) in Northeastern Rajasthan, India.* Unpublished Ph.D. Dissertation. University of Pennsylvania.

Sankalia, H. D., S. B. Deo and Z. Ansari. 1969. *Excavations at Ahar (Tambavati).* Pune, Deccan College Post-Graduate and Research Institute.

Shinde, V. 2000. The origin and development of the Chalcolithic in Central India, *Indo-Pacific Prehistory Association Bulletin* 19, 125-36.

Shinde, V., G. L. Possehl and M. Ameri. 2005. Excavations at Gilund 2001-2003: The seal impressions and other finds. In U. Franke-Vogt and H-J. Weisshaar (eds), *South Asian Archaeology 2003*, 159-69. Aachen, Linden Soft Verlag.

Tripathi, A. 2000. *Recent Excavations in Rajasthan.* Jaipur, Archaeological Survey of India, Jaipur Circle.

Tripathi, A. 2001. *Archaeological Excavation at Ojiyana.* Jaipur, Archaeological Survey of India, Jaipur Circle.

Vishnu-Mittre. 1974. Climate vs. biotic factor: Pollen evidence in the postglacial history of Northwest India. In A. K. Ghosh, (ed.), *Perspectives in Paleoanthropology: Professor D. Sen Festschrift*, 25-31. Calcutta, Firma K. L. Mukhopadhyay.

www.ingramcontent.com/pod-product-compliance
Ingram Content Group UK Ltd.
Pitfield, Milton Keynes, MK11 3LW, UK
UKHW061214180426
11947UKWH00029B/2038